ON

GOLDMAN

Leslie A. Howe
University of Saskatchewan

Wadsworth
Thomson Learning™

Australia • Canada • Denmark • Japan • Mexico • New Zealand • Philippines
Puerto Rico • Singapore • Spain • United Kingdom • United States

Printed in the United States of America
1 2 3 4 5 6 7 03 02 01 00 99

For permission to use material from this text, contact us:
Web: www.thomsonrights.com
Fax: 1-800-730-2215
Phone: 1-800-730-2214

For more information, contact:
Wadsworth/Thomson Learning
10 Davis Drive
Belmont, CA 94002-3098
USA
www.wadsworth.com

ISBN: 0-534-57620-6

CONTENTS

1

Red Emma

If I can't dance, I don't want to be part of your revolution.

However it happens, certain phrases enter into common language that, although they may come with an otherwise bona fide set of credentials, were never, in fact, said by those who are famous for having said them. Particularly well known examples include Sherlock Holmes' "Elementary, my dear Watson", "Play it again, Sam" from the movie *Casablanca*, and even *Star Trek's* fairly infamous "Beam me up, Scotty". The "quotation" given at the beginning of this chapter is yet another in this collection of sayings that really ought to have been said but, alas, were not. What Emma Goldman actually did say was a great deal more elaborate, but the essential point is, perhaps, best expressed in the nutshell we could have wished she had given us instead.

The episode that inspired the motto is told early on in her autobiography, *Living My Life*. Goldman had begun to establish a reputation for herself as a speaker and activist, and was, at the time, deeply involved in the New York cloakmaker's strike. She also loved to go to the dances. On one of these occasions, a dreadfully serious young man took her aside and offered her the opinion that it was "undignified" for an agitator, someone who was on her way to becoming a force in the anarchist movement, to dance. "Certainly not with such reckless abandon, anyway". She let him know what she thought. In her own words, she

> told him to mind his own business, I was tired of having the
> Cause constantly thrown into my face. I did not believe that
> a Cause which stood for a beautiful ideal, for anarchism, for
> release and freedom from conventions and prejudice, should
> demand the denial of life and joy. I insisted that our Cause
> could not expect me to become a nun and that the movement
> should not be turned into a cloister. If it meant that, I did not
> want it. "I want freedom, the right to self-expression,
> everybody's right to beautiful, radiant things". Anarchism
> meant that to me, and I would live it in spite of the whole
> world–prisons, persecution, everything. Yes, even in spite of
> the condemnation of my own closest comrades I would live
> my beautiful ideal.[1]

Although the story as Goldman herself tells it has a certain tendentious quality, it does capture a truly vital element in Goldman's understanding of anarchist theory and practice. It is simply this: what is the point, after all, of a social revolution? Clearly, it must be to make people's lives *better*. And that *must* include, alongside such obvious necessities as justice and freedom, the less well defended ones of beauty and pleasure, even the simple pleasures of fresh flowers and an evening's dancing. Goldman, though no slouch in the revolutionary cause, was never one to sacrifice the people to their salvation. Unlike the Bolsheviks whom she encountered in revolutionary Russia, she never lost sight of the fact that a theoretically sound structure of food distribution was of little value if the people had no bread to eat. And she had little praise for any system of life that granted only that: subsistence could not be enough; we must have joy as well.

Early Days

Emma Goldman may not always have been consistent in her theorizing, honest in her self-reporting, or detailed in laying out her vision of the anarchist future, but there can be no question that she lived her life in dedication to the anarchist cause. This was not the armchair speculation of a revolutionary dilettante. True, Red Emma was not to be found on the barricades, but the anarchist reconstruction of society that Goldman stood for is one that requires individual transformation through the sharing of ideas and experiences and a lot of fairly tedious day to day ground level effort, such as she performed as a nurse and midwife, enabling over-delivered working women to obtain vital information about contraception at a time when imparting such information was illegal. Not the stuff of grand socialist opera, but anarchism is a way of life that demands unity of thought and deed. For Goldman, the anarchist revolution and the journey of her life were inseparable.

Emma Goldman's autobiography, *Living My Life*, (fittingly, perhaps) is a large and often frustrating document, and it is less a disclosure of herself than an itinerary of her revolutionary development and actions. Nevertheless, it and her report of her two year sojourn in post-revolutionary Russia offer a fascinating window into turn of the century revolutionary events, and the conditions that gave them impetus.

Emma Goldman was born in Kovno (Kaunas, Lithuania), on 27 June 1869. She had very little in the way of formal education: a few years while the family lived in Königsberg from 1875-81. She endured a childhood that was not exactly miserable, but very often harsh and unhappy. She had a tendency to stand up for herself that frequently brought her severe beatings from her embittered and commercially inept father. At the age of sixteen, she and her stepsister Helena escaped the bleakness of their life in Russia when they were at last permitted to emigrate to America, joining their older sister Lena in Rochester, New York.

As had so many before her, young Emma soon found that America was not quite the Promised Land after all. It was clear that it would be difficult for her sister to provide for yet more mouths, and she set about finding work. It was a disillusioning experience. Even in so-called "model" factories, the conditions bordered on the Dickensian. The work was hard and ludicrously underpaid, given the profits that were evidently being made.

Emma found Rochester a constraining environment, that gradually became suffocatingly claustrophobic. She was attracted at first to a young man, Jacob Kershner, originally from Odessa, who seemed interested in books and with whom she could speak Russian. She soon found that he was actually fairly dull, but she was lonely and needed companionship.

The rest of the Goldman family arrived in late Fall of 1886; anti-Semitism was high in St. Petersburg and the amount of bribery required to stay in business had outstripped Goldman's father's means.

With her parents, two younger brothers, Helena, and Emma in one house it was still difficult to make ends meet, and Kershner was taken on as a boarder. The combination of lack of privacy and having Kershner in such proximity kept Emma in a state of some tension. She had come to realize that she really didn't like him very much, but he was there, the only person other than family whom she knew, and she needed someone. They were married in February 1887, in accord with Jewish rites.[2]

The marriage grew increasingly insufferable, due to their growing incompatibility and Jacob's impotence. They were divorced ten months later and Emma left for New Haven, where she worked in a corset factory and made the acquaintance of anarchist and socialist radicals. Having to return to Rochester some time later, she almost immediately met up with Kershner, who pleaded with and badgered her into remarrying him. She did so and stuck it out for another three months, until she could stomach it no more and left him for the last time, to the very great disapproval of her parents and the local Jewish community.[3]

Goldman had already been introduced to some hint of revolutionary ideas during the brief period that the family resided in St. Petersburg. These were tumultuous times, with nihilist plots and assassination attempts on the Tsar. She felt a deep sympathy for those whose own sympathy with suffering impelled them to sacrifice themselves, and she drank in the stories of Russian revolutionist women in particular. But it was the Haymarket incident that truly galvanized her incipient revolutionism.

Haymarket

The 1880's were not a good time to be a worker. There was significant industrial expansion going on, but little if any sense of social responsibility on the part of industrialists towards the labour force that was making them extremely rich. Labour organizations began to be formed and workers struggled to form unions and even the most insignificant of legal protection. There was grinding poverty, even for those who worked long hours under appalling conditions. And when a worker was sucked dry, he or she could expect to be tossed away like an empty rind.

In May of 1886 strikes were organized to agitate for the eight hour working day. The centre of this movement was Chicago, and the May 1 demonstrations there, although peaceful, excited very hostile press and denunciations by business leaders. A conflict between strikers and scabs at the McCormick Harvester Company two days later resulted in the deaths of two of the workers. A meeting was held the next day, 4 May, to protest police brutality. Those who spoke, including some prominent Chicago anarchists (Albert Parsons, August Spies, and Adolph Fischer), defended the workers and the eight hour day, but there was no advocacy of violent action and it was a peaceable meeting. However, as the meeting wound down, a body of police appeared and ordered the crowd dispersed immediately, though a few speakers remained. As the police were laying about with their clubs, a bomb was tossed in their direction, leaving seven dead, along with some number of onlookers.

There was a huge public uproar against the agitators, which was largely directed against the anarchists. The outcry was vindictive and xenophobic. It was as if war had been declared against the anarchists, who, so far as anyone could positively tell, were not actually connected to the bombing. Nevertheless, eight prominent anarchists were arrested for the incident, and faced what was to all intents and purposes, a show trial. Parsons, Spies, Fischer, Louis Lingg, and George Engel were given the death penalty; two others were sentenced to life imprisonment and a third to fifteen years.[4]

This incident had an extraordinary effect on Goldman and on a great many other sympathetic observers. Again and again, she tells of meeting radicals who had become so because of the Haymarket martyrs.

The event served as a turning point for the development of radicalism in the United States. In Goldman's case, it was during the Haymarket trial that she came across an issue of *Die Freiheit*, a German-language paper edited by Johann Most, which was filled with news about what was transpiring in Chicago. She was blown away by the passion in the prose. She had to read more, everything she could about anarchism and about the men on trial. With the tremendous shock of the executions, she made up her mind to dedicate herself to the cause.

> *I had a distinct sensation that something new and wonderful had been born in my soul. A great ideal, a burning faith, a determination to dedicate myself to the memory of my martyred comrades, to make their cause my own, to make known to the world their beautiful lives and heroic deaths....*
>
> *My mind was made up. I would go to New York, to Johann Most. He would help me prepare myself for my new task.*[5]

Twenty-one months later and twenty years old, she arrives in New York on 15 August 1889, with five dollars, a sewing-machine, and three addresses, one of which is the office of *Die Freiheit*. She finds a young anarchist acquaintance she had made in New Haven, A. Solotaroff, who immediately introduces her to radical New York. Right away she encounters the eighteen year old Alexander Berkman, whose life will be entwined with hers for the next forty-seven years, and that same evening Berkman introduces her to Most.

Goldman's early relationship with Berkman was a fairly prickly one; he had a tendency to be solemn about self-sacrifice–spending money on things of beauty, such as music, art, theatre, or even fresh flowers, of which Goldman was very fond, seemed to him to be unrevolutionary. They argued frequently about Most as well, sometimes about his ideas, more often about Most's extravagances of food, drink, and theatre, which he occasionally shared with Goldman. As Goldman became closer to the older man, both Berkman and Most displayed a tendency to be extra critical of each other, which made life slightly awkward for Goldman.

Goldman and Berkman became lovers, while Most continued to exert an enormous intellectual force on her developing views. Johann Most had been a political activist in Germany and Austria and had spent various terms in prison for agitation, as well as serving briefly in the

German parliament. His radical credentials as a socialist, then, were well established before he came to America, where he quickly consolidated the German speaking social revolutionary movement. His advocacy of political violence earned him a great deal of police scrutiny and several periods of imprisonment.

At this period, Goldman found herself the object of much of Most's attention. She drank in eagerly all that he had to offer, from anarchist theory to French opera. As she says,

> *He opened up a new world to me, introduced me to music, books, the theatre. But his own rich personality meant far more to me—the alternating heights and depths of his spirit, his hatred of the capitalist system, his vision of a new society of beauty and joy for all.*
> *Most became my idol. I worshipped him.*[6]

Listening to her speak of her childhood experiences, Most was convinced that Goldman would make a powerful public speaker, and was determined to set her on that course. Goldman was a great deal less certain of her abilities. Whenever she had tried to speak up before, to ask a question from the floor, she would "experience a kind of sinking sensation. While I was listening to the speakers, the questions would formulate themselves easily enough, but the moment I got up on my feet, I would feel faint."[7] When she had attempted to make short speeches she felt utterly incompetent, though others told her she had come across as calm and controlled. She dreaded the prospect of an entire tour of speaking engagements that Most was setting up for her. She thought that if she simply memorized the notes with which Most had provided her, that would be enough on which to get by. She soon found that that was not going to do.

Several points were pressed home to her by her first speeches (on the subject of the futility of fighting for the eight hour day): that she could indeed speak to a crowd, with passion and eloquence; that Most's words were not hers; that she had to find her own voice and address the issues as she saw them.

7

> *I realized that I was committing a crime against myself and*
> *the workers by serving as a parrot repeating Most's*
> *views....My first public experience did not bring the result*
> *Most had hoped for, but it taught me a valuable lesson. It*
> *cured me somewhat of my childlike faith in the infallibility of*
> *my teacher and impressed on me the need of independent*
> *thinking.*[8]

Most did not appreciate the change in his little Emma. Goldman realized that he thought of her as "a mere female", someone who should simply be his mouthpiece, and a sexual object. They quarrelled fiercely, but remained comrades.[9] Nevertheless, the animosity between Most and Berkman became more pronounced. Most connived at packing Berkman off to Russia so that he could have Goldman to himself; he made clear his essentially sexual desire for Goldman (which, for all her affection for him, was not reciprocated).[10] Still, there was no deep break between the two until Goldman and Berkman both became involved with a rival revolutionist faction that published a periodical that went by the title of *Autonomie*. The appeal for Goldman was in its more individualist stance: it was a much more decidedly anarchist group than the more socialist *Freiheit*. But as far as Most was concerned, she had joined his enemies.[11]

Homestead

The strike at the Carnegie-owned steel mills in Homestead, near Pittsburgh, Pennsylvania, seemed to Goldman and Berkman to be a prime case for social revolutionist concern, and to present the ideal opportunity to advance the anarchist cause. It was also something of a personal disaster for the both of them. In many ways, the episode stands as a particularly telling tragicomedy of revolutionist naiveté.

Thanks to protectionist tariffs, the American steel industry was at the time experiencing a boom in prices and production, and the Carnegie Steel Company, which had its largest mills in Homestead, was fortunate enough to have a near monopoly. The Amalgamated Association of Iron and Steel Workers also happened to be one of the largest and most solid

8

labour organizations in the country. Worker's wages were on a sliding scale, indexed to steel prices. With their collective agreement nearly up, the workers were looking for a wage increase to reflect the current higher prices and production levels. With negotiations ongoing, Carnegie opted to leave the country for Scotland, leaving in charge the Company chairman, Henry Clay Frick. Frick cut off negotiation: there would be no more indexation and no more collective agreement. From now on, the Company would determine wages entirely on its own, and would negotiate with workers strictly on an individual basis. He would close the mills altogether, thereby terminating all employees, and start over with a whole new round of hiring. The Homestead mill would not be struck; the workers would be locked out instead.[12]

In a steel town, this move was bound to be highly unpopular, and Frick took a beating in the press. The steelworkers were defiant.

At this time, Goldman and Berkman were in Worcester, running an ice cream parlour. The idea was to raise enough funds to enable them to go back to Russia and advance the revolution in their homeland. However, the events in Homestead caught their attention, and they watched intently as events unfolded. To them, the way that the steelworkers were refusing to be cowed into submission seemed like the beginning of a worker revolt. And then one day, as Goldman was serving a gentleman in the shop, her glance caught the headline of the newspaper he was reading. The families of strikers were being evicted from their homes–a pregnant woman carried out into the street by the sheriffs–Frick refusing to concede anything to the workers and threatening to import Pinkerton detectives.[13]

Goldman and Berkman were consumed with revolutionary fervour. They were suddenly convinced that, being internationalists, they belonged in Homestead, not Russia. As Berkman argues, "We must bring [the workers] our great message and help them see that it was not only for the moment that they must strike, but for all time, for a free life, for anarchism."[14] So, they sell their shop, pack up, and head back to New York to get ready for their mighty blow against capitalism.

First, they decide that they must get a manifesto printed up to be distributed to the workers. This plan hits a bit of a snag when they realize that neither of them can write English. But they can find someone to do this for them, and then Goldman will address meetings of the workers, with German and English texts being distributed.

But then events take a fateful turn. The Homestead mills had been fortified and enclosed within a high fence. On 6 July, in the middle of the night, barges carrying (it was thought) strikebreakers and a contingent of armed Pinkertons made their stealthy way up the Monongahela River towards the mill. This move had been anticipated by the steelworkers and they moved to block any landing. There was a pitched battle, during which the Pinkertons opened fire, killing nine of the workers and a small boy, and wounding many others.[15] Seven of the Pinkertons were also killed. The militia was called out to restore order.

There was immediate outcry from the mainstream press and even from government.

As for the revolutionaries, Goldman and Berkman realized that their manifesto would be inadequate. Instead, they felt certain that this was the crucial moment in which they had to make a principled and decisive stand.

> *It was the psychological moment for an* Attentat; *the whole country was aroused, everybody was considering Frick the perpetrator of a coldblooded murder. A blow aimed at Frick would re-echo in the poorest hovel, would call the attention of the whole world to the real cause behind the Homestead struggle. It would also strike terror in the enemy's ranks and make them realize that the proletariat of America had its avengers.*[16]

They resolve to manufacture a bomb, although they have really no idea how to do this. The plan is to use a timed detonator, allowing Sasha to kill Frick and yet surrender himself, so that he can use his day in court to propagandize the cause. Evidently, they forgot once again that he couldn't speak English. In any event, the bomb building is unsuccessful, and they have to figure out how to get a gun instead.

While Berkman takes off for Pittsburgh, Goldman works on the problem of scraping together enough money for the venture. One morning she awakes with the solution: inspired by the example of Sonya in Dostoyevsky's *Crime and Punishment*, she will sacrifice her body as Sasha will his freedom—she will become a prostitute. This, too, is largely unsuccessful–she just doesn't have the nerve for it. She does, however, attract the attention of an older gentleman, who points out her unsuitableness for the profession, but gives her ten dollars to go home with. She borrows another fifteen dollars from her sister Helena, claiming illness, and sends it off after Berkman.[17]

On 23 July Alexander Berkman carries out his attempt on the life of Henry Clay Frick. While getting off three shots and stabbing him in the leg with a poisoned dagger, Berkman still only manages to wound Frick, and is himself immediately apprehended.

Goldman had been expecting there to be all kinds of acclaim for the act, as if the assassination would be the clarion call to revolution. She was shocked and disappointed to discover that the response was, on the whole, negative. The *Autonomie* group was elated, but aside from that, opinion, both public and revolutionist, went against Berkman. Johann Most, the terrorist of old, was dismissive of the effort, and even cast aspersions on its author's authenticity. Disagreement over the appropriateness of Berkman's Attentat ultimately split the anarchist community between the *Autonomie* and *Freiheit* camps. Goldman was particularly annoyed with Most's new found pacifism and, at one point, even bought a horsewhip and thrashed him with it in public.[18]

In the meantime, Goldman was persona non grata and, unable to find a room elsewhere, ended up living in what she eventually discovered to be a brothel.

Berkman was determined to defend himself at his trial, which did not go at all well. He was competent neither in English nor the law, and it was clear that he could not but be convicted. It was the sentence that stunned both Berkman and Goldman, for he was given twenty-two years when they had expected no more than seven.

Building for the Revolution

In the ensuing years, while continuing to work for the commutation of Berkman's sentence, Goldman also got on with her personal and revolutionary development. Key in this was a period of incarceration of her own.

11

In 1893, Goldman marched at the head of a demonstration on behalf of the unemployed, carrying a red banner–which was responsible for her gaining the nickname of "Red Emma". A meeting was held in Union Square at which she was to speak. Faced with the huge and fractious crowd, she abandoned her notes, which now seemed much too remote and irrelevant. Extemporizing on the words of Cardinal Manning, she finished her speech with the perhaps unfortunate words:

> *demonstrate before the palaces of the rich; demand work. If they do not give you work, demand bread. If they deny you both, take bread. It is your sacred right!*[19]

It was a thunderous success with the crowd and it got her arrested for incitement to riot.

Although defended by former New York mayor A. Oakey Hall, Goldman was convicted and sentenced to a year's imprisonment in the Blackwell's Island Penitentiary.

It was, in a way, all to the good, for it was in prison that Goldman was able to develop skills that would be invaluable to her through the following years. For one thing, she had not up to this time become at all proficient in English. Now, however, she had at once the time, the opportunity, and the necessity of learning the language. She was also able to read a great deal, broadening her acquaintance with works of literature which constant immersion in anarchist activism made difficult to do. Also, by being removed from the perpetual foment and partisanship of ideas for a time, she had a chance to gradually work her way towards her own path. And, in a more practical vein, she was able to learn an employable skill, one that would put her in a position both to learn more about actual social conditions and to do something about them.

The Penitentiary "was fortunate" to be without a staff physician. This meant that medical care was provided by the nearby Charity Hospital, which was a teaching hospital, overseen by a visiting physician from New York, a Dr. White. Dr. White, it seems, was a decent man. Whatever the case, the prison also lacked a permanent trained nurse. Dr. White persuaded Goldman to take up the work under his guidance and she spent the rest of her time learning the vocation.

In the end, as she herself put it,

The prison had been the crucible that tested my faith. It had helped me to discover strength in my own being, the strength to stand alone, the strength to live my life and fight for my ideals, against the whole world if need be. The State of New York could have rendered me no greater service than by sending me to Blackwell's Island Penitentiary![20]

After her release, she began to work as a practical nurse, working several hours a day in Dr. White's office, seeing private patients referred to her by another doctor, and in the new Beth-Israel Hospital on East Broadway. She loved her new profession and was able to earn more than she ever had before. She no longer had to endure the grind of sitting at a machine all day, and she had time both for reading and for activism.[21] However, she still needed more formalized training. Thus, in August of 1895, she left for England, en route to the Allgemeines Krankenhaus in Vienna for training in nursing and midwifery.[22]

While in England, aside from trying out her stuff at Speaker's Corner in Hyde Park, she was able to meet such great social revolutionaries as Petr Kropotkin, Enrico Malatesta (though they were not actually able to communicate), and Louise Michel, a heroine of the Paris Commune.

It was in Vienna that Goldman discovered the works of Friedrich Nietzsche, of whom she says that the "magic of his language, the beauty of his vision, carried me to un-dreamed-of heights....The fire of his soul, the rhythm of his song, made life richer, fuller, and more wonderful for me."[23]

Perhaps equally significant for the development of Goldman's views was her attendance at the lectures of the young Sigmund Freud. In this case, it was to her as if she had suddenly gained a clarity into subjects that had before been dim and clouded. "For the first time I grasped the full significance of sex repression and its effect on human thought and action. He helped me to understand myself, my own needs..."[24]

Back in the States, Goldman returned to work, this time taking on midwife cases. It was not lucrative, but it gave her valuable experience of the not-just-theoretical living conditions of the poor. What she reports as making a particularly forceful impression upon her is the desperate desire of poor women to avoid frequent pregnancies. They lived "in continual dread of conception,"[25] and when they became pregnant they would resort to all sorts of ridiculous or violent and dangerous means of self-abortion. So many of the children who were born to them died in infancy; many of those that survived were sickly and unwanted. They would beg her to abort them, but although she knew how, she had no faith in her ability to do so safely, and always refused.[26]

These experiences convinced her of the immediate need for some kind of solution. This was only reinforced by the attitudes of the doctors with whom she consulted about the problem. The excuses she was given were all fairly typical ones: "The poor have only themselves to blame; they indulge their appetites too much"; children were "the only joy the poor had"; in the future, when woman "uses her brains more, her procreative organs will function less." She thought it unjust to expect women and children, upon whom so much of the burden fell, to wait for that wonderful day.[27]

In 1899, she returned to Europe, having been sponsored to study medicine. She also continued with her anarchist activities and acquired a new lover. When one of her backers heard of this, he wrote to her that he was not interested in supporting her in such endeavours: "I am interested only in E.G. the woman—her ideas have no meaning whatever to me. Please choose." She did. In reply, she wrote: "E.G. the woman and her ideas are inseparable. She does not exist for the amusement of upstarts, nor will she permit anybody to dictate to her. Keep your money."[28]

Although she had with that abandoned the study of medicine, she had not abandoned her concerns with sexual issues and with contraception. While in Paris, she attended a necessarily clandestine Neo-Malthusian Congress, where she was able to receive some much needed material and moral support for her work in America.[29]

Czolgosz and McKinley

In the meantime, Goldman continued to give speeches and go on lecture tours across the United States. She was all of thirty-two years old and proving a very popular draw. Until 1901.

In September of that year, President William McKinley was assassinated by Leon Czolgosz, who declared himself an anarchist. Although Czolgosz denied that she had any involvement in or knowledge of his actions, the press linked Goldman's name to the assassination. The police were searching for her and holding friends of hers in Chicago until she was found. She determined to go to Chicago to give herself up, though most of her friends in New York and Chicago told her that would be nuts and she should escape to Canada. In any event she was arrested.

Goldman was kept incommunicado for several days. The police made every effort to get her to confess to having inspired Czolgosz, and to having financed him. Although it was five days before she received any friendly communication from the outside world, the police saw to it that plenty of hate-mail, mostly anonymous, got delivered to her.

> *"You damn bitch of an anarchist," one of them read, "I wish I could get at you. I would tear your heart out and feed it to my dog." "Murderous Emma Goldman," another wrote, "you will burn in hell-fire for your treachery to our country." A third cheerfully promised: "We will cut your tongue out, soak your carcass in oil, and burn you alive." The description by some of the anonymous writers of what they would do to me sexually offered studies in perversion that would have astounded authorities on the subject.[30]*

Anti-anarchist hysteria had flamed up all over again and found its lightning rods in both Czolgosz and Goldman. What did not help to dissipate the rage directed towards Goldman was the circumstance that she would not condemn Czolgosz for his actions, even though she now rejected such acts of violence. To her, he was

> *a creature at bay. Millions of people are ready to spring on him and tear him limb from limb. He committed the act for no personal reasons or gain. He did it for what is his ideal: the good of the people. That is why my sympathies are with him.[31]*

15

Yet, at the same time, now that McKinley was suffering and near death, he was simply another human being to her, and on that ground she would care for McKinley as a nurse if called upon to do so. The only clear criticism she actually makes of Czolgosz's act is to question his choice of target. A President is not the most direct representative of the machinery of capitalist oppression and exploitation. However, she concludes, he must have chosen McKinley because of the President's record as an instrument of American capitalist imperialism, beginning with the annexation of the Philippines, and continuing with his willingness to send troops in to support owners against strikers.[32]

In the end, the authorities in Buffalo, where McKinley was shot and where Czolgosz was being held, could not produce sufficient evidence of Goldman's involvement to support their case for extradition, and the charges had to be dropped after a month of detention and wrangling.

Public feeling against Goldman, however, remained high. And it was impossible for her to organize a meeting to speak on his behalf or to raise funds for his defence–no one, save Goldman, was willing to defend him in public. Even Berkman, to her very great dismay, rejected Czolgosz's act on the grounds that McKinley was not a real oppressor (unlike Frick), and thus that the "necessary social background" (essentially, economic, as opposed to purely political, injustice) was missing to justify the Attentat.[33] Most of the American and the Jewish anarchists would not recognize Czolgosz as being an anarchist at all. The French, Italian, and Spanish groups, on the other hand, were sympathetic, but they could not reach the English speaking American audience.[34]

Czolgosz was convicted, despite being blessed with not one, but two, court appointed and obviously reluctant defence lawyers, and was executed by the electric chair on 29 October 1901.

Birth Control

In March 1906 Goldman at last launched something she had dreamed of: *Mother Earth*, a periodical intended to put together her two passions of revolutionary social ideals and revolutionary ideas in artistic expression. Finally, her words would no longer have only that ephemeral quality of speech; the printed word could have a fuller effect, and she could be the conduit through which the ideas of young artists would gain expression, without fear of censorship. The proceeds of her American and Canadian lecture tours now went to support the magazine, once the anti-anarchist frenzy that had followed McKinley's assassination slowly quieted down.

Then in May 1906 Alexander Berkman was released from prison, after having served fourteen years. The reunion was difficult and he found readjusting to life outside of prison extremely challenging. The way Goldman saw it, Sasha's picture of her and of their relationship had remained stalled in 1892. In the meantime, she had matured and acquired her own ideas, her independence, her own life. They were not to be lovers again, but they were, for all their difficulty in getting along, forever bound up with each other.

Since her return to the States from the Paris Neo-Malthusian conference in 1900, Goldman had included birth control as one of the topics in her lecture series. She was not, however, quite as forward in her promotion of the issue as she might have been. Her reasoning was that this was one of many important concerns, but not the one she was willing to risk arrest for. She was constantly on the edge of arrest anyway; this didn't seem to be the red flag she wanted to wave in front of the bull of the State. If she was asked for specific information on contraception, in a private capacity, she would give it, but publicly she was circumspect and general.

However, by 1915, Margaret Sanger's difficulties in circulating her publication *The Woman Rebel*, and William Sanger's arrest for giving his wife's pamphlet on birth control to an undercover agent, changed Goldman's mind about how seriously she should be treating the issue.[35]

She determined to test the resolve of the authorities by speaking out directly. The forum was an audience of some six hundred people at the Sunrise Club in New York. Goldman, as was her wont, took care to take a book with her to read in jail, which is where she expected to spend the night. Despite giving what she describes as a frank discussion of contraceptive methods, there was no arrest.[36]

This not having roused the official guardians of public morals, she decided to deliver the same talk at her regular Sunday meeting. Still no reaction. It was not until after her next tour, when she made the subject a central part of her lectures to the women on the East Side that winter, that she finally was arrested. In response, a large protest meeting was held at Carnegie Hall, with many prominent speakers discussing the issue.[37]

The trial began on 20 April 1916, with Goldman pleading her own case and looking forward to the opportunity to give a defence of birth control in open court. As she tells it, she "spoke for an hour, closing with the declaration that if it was a crime to work for healthy motherhood and happy child-life, I was proud to be considered a criminal."[38] She was sentenced to fifteen days or a $100 fine; she refused to pay the fine and served what was to her an insignificant term.

All this had exactly the desired effect. There were now protests across the country and women taking it upon themselves to organize the distribution of contraception information. The issue had moved out of the realm of purely theoretical discussion and into that of direct action, with believers in birth control advancing the cause in practice and taking the consequences in terms of arrest and imprisonment. In the ensuing months, Goldman was arrested again, at various times and in various cities, as was Margaret Sanger, and many others.[39]

By 1917, Goldman was ready to leave this particular field of battle, on the grounds that she was satisfied with her contribution, but perhaps also because it had grown out of her grasp. "We were ready now to leave the field to those who were proclaiming birth-control as the only panacea for all social ills. I myself had never considered it in that light; it was unquestionably an important issue, but by no means the most vital one."[40]

No Conscription

As of 1917, the Great War had been going on for some time for Europeans, Canadians, and Australians. Eventually, America would join in as well. Once the U.S. did declare war, many of those who had supported the anti-war effort disappeared, and the work of maintaining the movement fell on the shoulders of the more radical contingent. This almost immediately became a fight over conscription.

Goldman was never, in the strictest sense, a pacifist, but conscription offended against her beliefs in the profoundest possible way. She declared of President Woodrow Wilson that the

academic author of The New Freedom *did not hesitate to
destroy every democratic principle at one blow. He had
assured the world that America was moved by the highest
humanitarian motives, her aim being to democratize
Germany. What if he had to Prussianize the United States in
order to achieve it? Free-born Americans had to be forcibly
pressed into the military mould, herded like cattle, and
shipped across the waters to fertilize the fields of France.
Their sacrifice would earn them the glory of having
demonstrated the superiority of* My Country, 'Tis of Thee
over Die Wacht am Rhein. *No American president had yet
succeeded in so humbugging the people as Woodrow Wilson,
who wrote and talked democracy, acted despotically,
privately and officially, and yet managed to keep up the myth
that he was championing humanity and freedom.*[41]

A conference was to be called in the *Mother Earth* office in order
to organize an anti-conscription league and to draw up a manifesto
condemning this measure which they saw as the greatest possible menace
to human rights and freedom of conscience. The question had to be
settled as to whether this No-Conscription League would actively
advocate nonregistration by eligible men. Goldman's position was that
as a woman, and therefore not directly affected by a draft order, she could
not legitimately advise someone who was so affected as to what they
personally should do. It was a matter of individual conscience, and a
self-respecting anarchist could not presume to determine another's
decision. But she would certainly defend the cause of anyone who
refused military service. This position was also adopted by the League.[42]

The first mass meeting was on 18 May at the Harlem River Casino,
and was attended by almost ten thousand people, including many newly
minted soldiers and a few hundred police and detectives.[43] Branches of
the League sprang up in other American cities. Goldman and company
strained their meagre financial resources to put out an extra large issue
of *Mother Earth* in order to get their message out to as wide an audience
as possible. They wanted to mail a copy to every Federal officer and
editor, as well as to get it widely distributed among young workers and
college students. As it happened, they needn't have worried; in their

effort to condemn the anti-conscriptionists, the mainstream New York press had already printed large excerpts from the group's manifesto, sometimes all of it. Now they reprinted much of the June issue, as well as publicizing the next scheduled mass meeting.

The 4 June meeting attracted a great deal of attention, especially from the police, who completely surrounded the hall and did their best to keep those who wished to attend outside. Gathered inside the hall were "officials from the Department of Justice, members of the Federal attorney's office, United States marshals, detectives from the 'Anarchist Squad', and reporters. The scene looked as if set for bloodshed."[44] The meeting was seriously disrupted by claqueurs who tossed light bulbs onto the stage. Jack Reed's request to the police captain that the trouble makers be tossed was denied. The meeting verged on the riotous and, in order to prevent the police getting the opportunity they were looking for, it was eventually brought to a close, with the singing of the *Internationale*.[45]

After this, most hall managers were intimidated into refusing to allow Goldman or Berkman to speak at their venues. Before a meeting at the only hall that would rent to them, Goldman received an anonymous telephone death threat. Since they had just received a $3,000 donation, she thought it advisable to make her will. The hall was packed and very lively. Everything went off very smoothly, but at the end of it, the police checked every man for his draft registration; those who had none were immediately arrested. It was evident that the meeting had been used by the police as a kind of stalking horse. Clearly, the League would have to change their tactics.[46]

However, the next afternoon, Goldman and Berkman were both arrested and charged with conspiracy against the draft. Goldman made use of her incarceration to rest and catch up on her reading with James Joyce's *Portrait of the Artist as a Young Man*.

Both Goldman and Berkman determined to have nothing to do with the farce of the law and refused to participate in their trial proceedings, and so they went in without a lawyer. They would only plead their own case, if necessary, in order to make their ideas heard. This they did, and were convicted, despite the fact that the very poorly supported charges were based on the 18 May meeting—which had taken place before the Conscription Law was signed into effect. They were each given the maximum penalty: two years in prison and a fine of ten thousand dollars.[47]

Goldman served the time in the Missouri Penitentiary, Berkman in Atlanta. She was released at the end of September in 1919, but was not free for long. Deportation proceedings began early in December. The sticking point was her marriage to Jacob Kershner, which was the basis of her claim to American citizenship. Kershner's citizenship had been revoked in 1909 (after he was already deceased) but it was only now that the Government made a serious move to deport Goldman. Held at Ellis Island, appeals proceeded as far as the Supreme Court, but all were denied and on 21 December 1919, Goldman, Berkman, and several hundred others were herded aboard a rusted old bucket of a ship, the *Buford*, and transported off towards Finland, and from thence by sealed train to Russia.

Russia

Almost from her arrival in revolutionary Russia, Goldman had the disturbing sense that all was not quite right with the revolution. St. Petersburg was not the vibrant city she had known so long ago, but its now meagre population was scrambling pathetically for food and fuel. There were the occasional gunshots in the night, although capital punishment had been abolished. She came across prostitutes selling themselves to soldiers for a little bread. It seemed inconceivable that there should be prostitution in revolutionary Russia, and food and lodging were supposed to have been requisitioned for the use of the people. Attending a meeting of the Petrograd Soviet, she was shocked to see the intolerant reaction to the request of a Menshevik to speak. Discussing the incident afterwards with her host, Zorin, she is told "Free speech is a bourgeois superstition...during a revolutionary period there can be no free speech."[48] What was going on?

There was a ready explanation for all this: the blockade, the presence of forces hostile to the success of the revolution: Western-backed White Guard insurrectionists, internal counter-revolutionary elements, and the like. Of course, in such a case, the revolution had to be nurtured and protected against those who would

21

see it turned back, and this required certain restrictions and impositions. Still, although Goldman found these explanations to be, on the face of things, logical and persuasive, she also had a slowly growing sense of their hollowness. Like someone trying not to acknowledge a distasteful personal truth, she tried to reconcile what she actually saw and experienced, and what she was told by ordinary people and by local anarchist activists, with the official story. "I was a newcomer...I had no right to judge," she told herself.[49] It did not seem possible, it was too difficult to believe, that the revolution she and so many others had so long hoped and worked for could be going so fundamentally astray.

There was an evident black market thriving. She tried to put it down to three years of war, and the fact that the Tcheka drew a percentage could be easily explained by the natural tendency of policemen to graft.[50] Goldman raised some of her concerns in a conversation with Maxim Gorki, questions about a plan to incarcerate "morally defective" children (the offspring of alcoholic or syphilitic parents), about political persecution and terror. Gorki had previously been extremely critical of the Bolsheviks. Now he simply said that the Bolsheviks were making some mistakes but doing the best they knew how.[51]

Moscow she found hierarchical and the people largely self-absorbed. But it was a much more alive place and the markets, especially, were a place where she could meet and talk with a wide range of people, who seemed to be quite skeptical about the truly revolutionary character of those who were, in effect, their new masters.

Local anarchists were extremely critical of the Bolsheviks. At a conference of the Moscow Anarchists in March, she heard how the anarchists had been instrumental in bringing about the Revolution, and that many were working hard in the Foreign Office and elsewhere. Nevertheless, five months after the October Revolution, the Anarchist Club had been machine gunned and their press suppressed. Many anarchists were imprisoned.[52]

She tried to raise her concerns in an interview with Lenin. Her impression of him was that he was a Puritan, a utilitarian, for whom things like free speech and "the spiritual achievements of centuries" were of little concern–he would use people as he needed them, and she wasn't entirely sure that it would be for the revolution.[53]

22

Visiting Kropotkin was no more encouraging. Kropotkin argued that the Bolsheviks had diverted the Revolution, using power to establish their own dictatorship at its expense. They had made the mistake of suppressing the cooperatives, which would have been able to bridge the interests of workers and peasants. The oppression and political persecution the Bolsheviks had engaged in had completely discredited socialism and communism to the people. But he could not bring himself to protest while Russia was being attacked by counter-revolutionists, and in any case, there was no forum in which to do so.[54]

For some months she looked for some positive way to contribute to the progress of the Revolution. She was involved for a time in the business of preparing for the arrival of another thousand Russian-American deportees. Despite the automatic apologetics blaming counter insurgents for all that seemed questionable, the corruption, interminable bureaucratic entanglements, Party favouritism, and the rest could not be brushed away and Goldman found herself becoming increasingly depressed at the sickly state of the Revolution she had so long hoped for.

Failing to find useful work to do with either the Ministry of Education or of Health (and unimpressed with the administration of either Department, as well as being unwilling to become part of the Communist machine that was becoming more and more distasteful to her), Goldman at last found the position she needed, attached to the Museum of the Revolution. She, Berkman, and a few others were charged with collecting material relevant to the Revolution (artifacts and data), and the Expedition was given the use of a railroad car, enabling it to travel from Petrograd and Moscow through the Ukraine to Odessa. This had the additional investigative advantage that it gave Goldman the opportunity to see a great deal of what was going on outside of the major city centres and to talk to individuals a little further outside of the stifling atmosphere of Petrograd.

Of the various people and groups she meets, it is her reaction to the situation of the Jews in the Ukraine that is among the most interesting, primarily for what it reveals of herself. Although certainly concerned with the persecution of the Jews, more than once she is inclined to dismiss their complaints about their treatment. There is an ambivalence in Goldman's attitude to Jewishness that comes out in her comments on these encounters. For example, after meeting with the Zionists of Poltava, she remarks that she felt

> *that the Zionist criticism of the Bolshevik regime was inspired by a narrow religious and nationalistic attitude. They were Orthodox Jews, mostly tradesmen whom the Revolution had deprived of their sphere of activity. Nevertheless, their problem was real—the problem of the Jew suffocating in the atmosphere of active anti-Semitism.*[55]

After meeting with members of the Jewish *Kulturliga* in Kiev, she comments that she thought that both those elder members who gave their cautious support to the Bolsheviks on the grounds that at least they had stopped the pogroms, and those younger ones who thought them too dangerous because they allowed physical survival but threatened cultural assimilation, "took a purely nationalistic view of the Russian situation." She was more concerned about the effects of the Revolution on Russia as a whole. How the Jews were treated was just one issue.[56]

And again, her assessment of a group of Zionists met in Odessa, who were concerned that Jewish culture was at risk of being obliterated under the Bolsheviks even if the Jews themselves were not, is that

> *These intellectual Jews were not part of the proletarian class. They were bourgeois without any revolutionary spirit. Their criticism of the Bolsheviki did not appeal to me for it was a criticism from the Right. If I had still believed in the Communists as the true champions of the Revolution I could have defended them against the Zionist complaints.*[57]

These and many other references Goldman makes to Jewish identity suggest that she herself did not have one. She saw being a Jew as a question of nationality above all. Her atheism would, of course, preclude a religious identification, and she has, it seems, little respect for any (or anyone's) religious adherence. As for herself, her various comments here and scattered throughout *Living My Life* suggest that she rarely, if ever, saw herself as having a Jewish identity. In fact, she speaks in one place of having long since shaken off her Jewish nationality. She claimed to be an internationalist, but her self-descriptions are almost always in terms of her Russian-ness, and secondarily as American (though this is usually her report of how others see her).

In the end, the experience of the Expedition really only helped to reinforce her disenchantment with the Bolshevik regime. But the final break with the Bolsheviks came with the slaughter of the anarchists at Kronstadt. The conflict had begun in February 1921, when the workers in a number of Petrograd factories went on strike–something that should not happen in a Communist state. A demonstration by the workers had been quite brutally broken up by the militia. The sailors of Kronstadt (the naval station just outside Petrograd) had always been among the staunchest supporters of the Revolution, having been pivotal in the Revolution of 1905 and in the storming of the Winter Palace in October 1917. But they were largely Anarchist, and bound to oppose Bolshevik tactics in suppressing the Petrograd strikers. They declared their solidarity with the strikers and organized a mass meeting in Kronstadt on 1 March, at which they called for, amongst other things, new Soviet elections by secret ballot, freedom of speech and assembly for workers, peasants, Anarchists, and left Socialists, liberation of leftist political prisoners, equal rations for those who work, and the abolition of political bureaus (so that no party should be given special propaganda privileges).[58]

At the meeting of the Petrograd Soviet three days later, the sailors' uprising was attributed to White influence, they were described as counterrevolutionists, and ordered to surrender or else be exterminated.[59] On March 7, bombardment of the fortress of Kronstadt began and by the 17th, the sailors had been "liquidated."[60]

This was the end for Goldman. She would no longer have anything to do with a murderous State and resolved to attempt to live independently. This stance was potentially a dangerous one for her to adopt, all the more so since Anarchists were now being arrested, imprisoned, and occasionally deported, but more often shot, at an accelerated pace. In time, plans were made to smuggle her out of the country. Fortuitously, however, a group of Berlin Anarchists requested that the Soviet Government issue passports for her, Berkman, and Alexander Shapiro, in order to attend the International Anarchist Congress in Berlin in December 1921, and they were permitted to leave.

Emma Goldman's criticism of the Russian Revolution comes down to two main points. First, that the Revolution, as carried out by the Bolsheviks, failed to address in an effective and concrete way those conditions that had been the original incentive to revolution. Simply, the

Bolsheviks failed to give the workers what would really have made a difference to their lives: better working conditions, more food, adequate housing, etc. A particularly telling example of the Bolshevik tendency to miss the point is illustrated by the story Goldman tells of the conditions of the women working in the Laferm tobacco plant. The atmosphere in the plant being stifling and oppressive, the women and young girls working there had attempted to obtain a rest room for themselves where they could go to eat their meals away from their workbenches, but the request was refused on the somewhat questionable grounds that there was no room to spare. Discussing what she had seen there later with Lisa Zorin, she argued

> *'But if even such small improvements had not resulted from the Revolution...what purpose has it served?' 'The workers have achieved control,' Lisa replied; 'they are now in power, and they have more important things to attend to than rest rooms–they have the Revolution to defend.' Lisa Zorin had remained very much the proletarian, but she reasoned like a nun dedicated to the service of the Church.*
>
> *The thought oppressed me that what she called the 'defence of the Revolution' was really only the defence of her party in power. At any rate nothing came of my attempt at social welfare work.*[61]

The second major thrust of Goldman's criticism is closely related to the first, and is largely directed to the Statist commitments of Bolshevism. For Goldman, it becomes clear that Russian Communism is antithetical to the goals of the original Revolution, that it is in fact counter-revolutionary, in methods and aims. As she put it, "the Revolution and the Bolsheviki, proclaimed as one and the same, were opposites, antagonistic in aim and purpose. The Revolution had its roots deep down in the life of the people. The Communist State was based on a scheme forcibly applied by a political party."[62] This quotation captures much of Goldman's objection to the Bolshevik co-opting of the Revolution: the Revolution was a popular initiative; the Bolshevik state was a top-down imposition by a particular political party over top of this original libertarian rejection of oppression, one which then assumed the authority for legitimizing all further expressions of revolutionary action, as a means of strengthening the power and position of the Communist Party. Moreover, whereas the methods of the Revolution in achieving its aim of emancipation were essentially libertarian, argues Goldman, those of the State (Bolshevik or otherwise) are inevitably those of coercion, leading in the course of things to oppression, violence, and terrorism.[63] If anything, the circumstances of the Russian Revolution prove two primary Anarchist principles: that ends and means are inseparable, and that the State cannot bring forth revolutionary change. As Goldman argues, "the Russian Revolution has demonstrated beyond doubt that the State idea, State Socialism, in all its manifestations (economic, political, social, educational) is entirely and hopelessly bankrupt. Never before in all history has authority, government, the State, proved so inherently static, reactionary, and even counter-revolutionary in effect. In short, the very antithesis of revolution."[64]

Thus, the Party and the Revolution were diametrically opposed, both in terms of ends and in terms of means. The Bolshevik ethic, according to Goldman, was that the end justifies the means. And the means employed by the Bolshevik State were in many ways unnecessarily and short-sightedly divisive and thus counterproductive. A case in point is the treatment of the intelligentsia. In *My Disillusionment in Russia*, Goldman tells of a tour of the Petropavlovsk Fortress (the notorious Czarist prison) and of seeing scrawled on a cell wall the statement "Tonight I am to be shot because I had once acquired an education."[65] The author had been one of many intellectuals shot or "disappeared" after the October Revolution. To Goldman, such a programme makes no sense at all. Everyone is needed for the successful reconstruction of society: scientists, engineers, researchers, teachers, and artists, just as much as carpenters, machinists, and farm workers.

> *Not hatred, but unity; not antagonism, but fellowship; not shooting, but sympathy–that is the lesson of the great Russian débâcle for the intelligentsia as well as the workers. All must learn the value of mutual aid and libertarian coöperation. Yet each must be able to remain independent in his own sphere and in harmony with the best he can yield to society. Only in that way will productive labour and educational and*

cultural endeavour express themselves in ever newer and richer forms.[66]

Implicit in this statement is an attitude to human existence that seems to mark in a truly fundamental way Goldman's rejection of Bolshevism: its disregard of and even contempt for the inwardly human. It is the view that the decisively human is not in the great constructions of civilization, whether these are monuments, political institutions, or even great exploits of science and exploration, but in the most basic of human feelings and motivations: not the hand but the heart, in a manner of speaking. And this, for Goldman, was the real failure of the Russian Revolution: those directing its unfolding changed only the superficial aspects of the State, ignoring the deep change in human and not just social values that had to go along with it.[67] Nevertheless, it did, as Goldman herself argues, attempt to override some very basic and (for Goldman) very important human values. As she laments, "Man's instinctive sense of equity was branded as weak sentimentality; human dignity and liberty became a bourgeois superstition; the sanctity of life, which is the very essence of social reconstruction, was condemned as un-revolutionary, almost counter-revolutionary. This fearful perversion of fundamental values bore within itself the seed of destruction."[68] Thus, the Bolshevik Revolution failed utterly to recognize the primary purpose of the social revolution, and in the process, violated the legitimizing goal of revolution itself. Not only did the Bolsheviks make the great mistake of thinking that the end justifies the means (whereas ends and means must be identical), but they had long since abandoned the end in favour of the means.

The ultimate end of all revolutionary social change is to establish the sanctity of human life, the dignity of man, the right of every human being to liberty and well-being. Unless this be the essential aim of revolution, violent social changes would have no justification.[69]

Latter Days

Goldman, Berkman, and Alexander Schapiro sat in Riga for some time waiting for their visas to enter Germany to arrive. As the delay continued, they were told that they would soon have to leave, no matter whether they had a visa into another country or not. Leave to go where? they asked. Back to your own country, they were informed. And where was that? The realization sunk in that they had no country.[70]

At the last minute, they received Swedish visas, sent to them by their syndicalist comrades in that country. This stay lasted only three and a half months, after which Goldman landed in Berlin. She set about writing the book that she had originally entitled *My Two Years in Russia*, but which appeared as *My Disillusionment in Russia*.

Goldman was caught in a no-win situation: to carry the anarchist cause was to risk expulsion; to criticize the Bolsheviks was to make her extremely unpopular with both true faith Communists and otherwise conservative governments attempting to normalize diplomatic relations with Soviet Russia. She would be vilified by all sides. And she was finding it difficult to find a secure place to live and work, not to mention income. She began to consider the merits of a marriage of convenience in order to establish citizenship rights somewhere. Eventually she ended up in England. Again, all would be well so long as she said nothing critical of Soviet Russia. There were those who were more sympathetic and willing to work with her, among them Rebecca West, Colonel Josiah Wedgwood, Bertrand Russell (who had accompanied the British Labour Mission to Russia), Harold Laski, but, save for West, even this support faded. No one wanted to help feed the reactionary cause, as they feared Goldman's criticism of the Bolsheviks would do.

The inertia of British political life and the grey dampness of the climate were wearing on Goldman. In June 1925, she married a Welsh coal miner and longtime anarchist comrade named James Colton. "British now, I did as most natives do who can scrape up enough to escape their country's climate."[71] She headed for the south of France. She spent several months there writing before heading off to Canada for an extensive and fairly successful lecture tour in 1926. Receiving a very friendly welcome in Toronto, as well as resources, she opted to stay for some time, returning to France in January of 1928 to write her autobiography.[72]

She was able to make lecture tours to Denmark and Sweden, and in 1934, she was permitted to enter the United States for ninety days, provided she limit her talks to drama and literature.

In June 1936, a despondent and ill Alexander Berkman committed suicide. Goldman was lost and uncertain of how to live. Then, three weeks later, revolution occurred in Spain, when the Fascists rebelled against the Leftist coalition that had won the elections in February of that year. Soon, she was asked to aid the defence of the Spanish Left. From England, she acted as a propagandist for the Loyalist cause.

Then, finally, on 17 February 1940, while in Toronto on a Canadian tour to raise money for the Loyalists, Emma Goldman suffered a stroke that left her paralyzed. She died three months later, on 14 May 1940.

2
Anarchism

Revolutionary Theory

Anarchism is usually thought of as one of those quintessentially late 19th century political movements that spawned bomb-throwers in Russia and the odd central European state, and furtive émigrés in London. It is associated with violence, nihilism, and godlessness. Many of the historical stereotypes hold a grain of truth; most are deeply misleading.

First, nihilists and anarchists are not the same being: anarchists reject the rule of authority; nihilists deny the legitimacy of all values. This puts nihilists and anarchists necessarily at odds, as the anarchist rejection of power is based on the assumption that there are indeed values that must be respected, and which are the ground of the demand for the revolution.

Anarchism is in many ways similar to Existentialism, not only in respect of the circumstance that they share many values and attitudes, but in the fact that it is just about as difficult and perhaps futile to characterize "*Anarchism*" as it is "*Existentialism*". There is no definitive programme or school of thought to which all adherents of either Anarchism or Existentialism adhere in all instances. The religious question is a prime case in point. Although it is true that the majority of anarchists, as with existentialists, tend to atheism, there have been profoundly Christian anarchist movements, just as some of the most notable existentialist thinkers have been religiously committed, as, e.g., Søren Kierkegaard and Martin Buber.

The Digger sect in 17th century England, represented in the works of Gerrard Winstanley, is a particularly intriguing instance of anarchistic Christianity; the great Russian novelist Leo Tolstoy is another, more well known, example. The Diggers (or "True Levellers") arose during that time of disruption and political, religious, and intellectual ferment, the English Civil War. They were a deeply Protestant sect that maintained the right of the people to agricultural use of traditional common lands in the face of heavy taxation and enclosure by property owners. Winstanley and his fellow Diggers believed in the justice of individual manual labour on the land and a communistic sharing of goods and property, and they managed to carry out their beliefs for a short time despite some fairly heavy handed opposition.

Tolstoy espoused a similar view as to the fundamental moral value of personal labour and saw social redemption as going through the individual's relationship to the divine. But he had little use for social movements aimed at the amelioration of material conditions.

Anarchism can also be distinguished into right-wing and left-wing varieties. In fact, it might be more accurate to say that the various kinds of Anarchism form a separate political spectrum. That is, from an anarchist perspective, right wing (Fascist) totalitarianism is not significantly different from the left wing (Leninist) variety, simply because both are fundamentally defined by the exclusive concentration and deployment of *power*. Anarchism, with its rejection of the legitimacy of power is the enemy of *both* positions, which it considers to be much more alike than opposed.

That aside, within Anarchism we can find "right wing" and "left wing" strains, those that place the greatest stress on individual expression and egoistic independence as absolute values that must in no way be infringed (libertarianism), and other traditions that emphasize the communitarian aspect of social existence (e.g., syndicalism).

For example, Max Stirner (Bavarian, 1806-1856), one of the "Young Hegelians", in his work *The Ego and His Own*, elaborates on the theme of the self-liberation and self-ownership of the individual ego. This is achieved through the rejection of the tyranny of absolute or conventional fixed concepts and of the imposition of any will at all upon the ego other than one's own–which is only one's own insofar as one has made it one's own and it is one's own at each present moment. Stirner's book is an exaltation of the individual ego above all others, of whatever kind. This goes so far as to include all thought, all concepts, all language, that is brought to the ego from outside of itself. The ego is prior to thought and must own its own thought: thinking "is nothing more than–*property*."[1] The question, then, is who is to own my thought: myself or some other. There is no absolute truth; "I am the criterion of truth."[2]

For Stirner, might is the basis of all freedom and right. There is only the freedom that one gets for oneself, and one can only do this with might; therefore, freedom is might (power). Thus far, Stirner's views, although delivered in a voice more like to Nietzsche than to Goldman, are not terribly far removed from many other anarchists. However, Stirner also wants to argue that self-interest is the fundamental motive of all human action, no matter how selfless and devotional it might appear to be. Indeed, that the Egoist is simply the supreme realist.[3] Now, if valuation is contingent upon self-interest (as Stirner claims), and if self-interest justifies force (as it seems it must), then force and the right are coincident. Self-ownership is dependent upon might or force; right is dependent upon self-ownership and self-interest; thus, right is a matter of might.[4] There is no absolute or independent Right, nor can one plausibly claim any kind of ideal Justice on this picture, either.

This puts Stirner outside the trend of most anarchist thinkers, and certainly outside the vast majority of anarchistic *movements*. After all, although there are many very good reasons to criticize absolutist systems of valuation, and anarchists are, by and large, deeply skeptical of such moralities, a social or political *movement* does have to be able to make inclusive claims with respect to justice, good, and the like–not only exclusively egoistic ones. Despite this, it is worth noting that Goldman was much impressed by both Stirner and Nietzsche. She was especially fond of Nietzsche, for what she saw as his extraordinarily poetic language, the modernness of his ideas, and his dedication to individual expression. She did not find many anarchists who shared her taste in this respect. On one occasion, in defending him against the charge of being elitist, she argued that he

> *was not a social theorist but a poet, a rebel and innovator. His aristocracy was neither of birth nor of purse; it was of the spirit. In that respect Nietzsche was an anarchist, and all true anarchists were aristocrats.*[5]

Goldman's individualism is a trait that put her somewhat at odds with other contemporary anarchists, who were readier than she to sacrifice the individual to the collective. Although the individual was not nearly so sacred to her as to Stirner, it is striking just how much emphasis she does put on it. She was highly critical of mass culture and the tendency of human beings to seek intellectual and moral security in numbers, and she believed that it would be "intelligent minorities" that would advance the anarchist cause and the development of art and culture. This might be seen as elitism, or it might instead indicate a realistic assessment of the power wielded by the manipulators of public opinion and taste, the capitalist economic and ideologic machine of consensus formation. There seems little point in denying what has been the despair of revolutionaries for centuries: that the people so rarely want it.

By contrast, Petr Kropotkin (Russian, 1842-1921) argues that the origin of the moral sentiment is sympathy, that the sense of solidarity is "the leading characteristic of all animals living in society", and far more important than competition.[6] Kropotkin was one of those who saw in science a means of combatting the entrenched injustices and hypocrisies of traditional moralities. In particular, he put his faith in evolutionary biology and tried to demonstrate, through works such as *Mutual Aid* and others, that it was cooperation, not brutal survival-of-the-fittest social carnage, that moved a species forward. Science, he thought, could provide ethics with concrete content.

Ethics is not immutable or transcendental, but always incomplete, a work in progress, constantly needing to be revised as the human species evolved.[7] Moral values have a natural social origin, and it is the basic impulse towards mutual aid that is responsible for our valuing benevolence and solidarity, which are in turn the basis of justice, equity, and self-sacrifice.[8] The task of ethics is to effect a synthesis (not a compromise) between the two contrary human tendencies towards mutual aid on the one hand, and mutual struggle on the other.[9]

> Mutual Aid–Justice–Morality *are thus the consecutive steps of an ascending series, revealed to us by the study of the animal world and man.* They constitute an organic necessity *which carries in itself its own justification, confirmed by the whole of the evolution of the animal kingdom, beginning with its earliest stages, (in the form of colonies of the most primitive organisms), and gradually rising to our civilized human communities. Figuratively speaking, it is a* universal law of organic evolution, *and this is why the sense of Mutual Aid, Justice, and Morality are rooted in man's mind with all the force of an inborn instinct...*[10]

Kropotkin's somewhat academic approach is perhaps a little unusual, but although his scientific orientation is outside the (nineteenth century) norm, his stress on mutuality and cooperation, sympathy and integration, are quite a bit truer to the overall anarchist tradition than Stirner's aggressive triumph of the individual will. It is no surprise that Goldman had such great regard for the old Anarchist Prince, whose acquaintance she had made in England, and whom she visited while in Russia in 1920-21.

Having remarked on all these differences, there are nevertheless a number of points that can be said to be central to (most) Anarchist thought. What helps to tie all these elements together is the fact that Anarchism is first and foremost an ethical position, rather than simply a political one–though to an anarchist the two are hardly separable. It is because of this moral underpinning that it makes sense for a political activist such as Mikhail Bakunin to argue that exploitation is the necessary consequence of the notion of morally independent individuals, in other words, "relations which, being motivated only by material needs, are not sanctioned nor backed up by some moral needs."[11] How these things interconnect may become clearer if we consider the three most fundamental elements of anarchism.

Autonomy

Anarchism rejects any form of power, authority, or domination. That includes not only state structures, law, and the police, but the less overt and often very subtle forms implied by intellectual authority, the persuasive influence of custom and social expectation, and many kinds of personal relationship (consider how many sorts of affectional or erotic relationships are based in systems of power and subordination of self, e.g., romantic love). The reason for rejecting power is not simply some vague immediate intuition that power is a bad thing, or even that the use or misuse of power by one group over another may lead to various kinds of nastiness–this is not a utilitarian view, which argues that domination of one group by another is bad because it makes one of those groups very unhappy. Anarchists may well agree with such an observation, but that is not why they reject authority. The most important value to an anarchist is autonomy (or freedom, but the term "autonomy" captures the anarchist sense much better–we are not talking only about political liberty here, though that certainly does enter into the picture later on). The individual must be free to choose for him or herself, to make choices that are definitively their own, and not that are pre-programmed for the individual to make. To be able to make truly free choices, one must be free not only in an external, negative, sense (unconstrained), but internally as well–one must be one's own person: one must be truly autonomous, untyrannized by false consciousness and the idols of social conformity or received doctrine. One must be able to possess oneself completely; one must not be controlled by another, or by alien structures of imperatives. One must be capable of fully determining oneself, and of being fully responsible for oneself.

Power, of course, seriously distorts the individual's ability to act autonomously. One cannot be free so long as institutions based on relations of power persist in society. (The best way to think of what anarchism is getting at is to think of the *power* of advertising, though nothing of that magnitude existed in the time of Goldman or Kropotkin, not even the Church.)

A consequence of this uncompromising attitude to power and autonomy is the anarchist assumption that one can only free oneself–one can never "free" other people. Someone who does not want to be free cannot live freely; they will throw their freedom away as quickly as possible. And the act of "freeing" someone actually puts them in your power; after all, they have to be grateful, don't they? More to the point, their freedom isn't theirs; they enter the life of freedom in a diminished state, uncertain of who they are, whether they really are free, ready to take someone else's "advice", and owing their freedom to someone else. (Think of the relationship that so often holds between Imperialist powers and their former colonies or protectorates.) As we shall see, this is something that Goldman insists upon with respect to women's emancipation--that they must emancipate themselves.[12]

Individual and Community

The second major point that anarchism insists upon is the inseparability of the link between the individual and the community.

Traditional liberal theory, as exemplified by classical thinkers such as John Locke and Jean-Jacques Rousseau, and present day authors of the likes of John Rawls, emphasizes the identity of the individual as an atomistic unit; when the individual chooses a course of action, they do so as if they were completely distinct from the rest of the society around them; in an important sense, individual and society are seen as opposites. This strain in liberalism is sometimes expressed in a relatively extreme form of libertarianism that rejects any governmental role beyond the most limited of caretaker functions and sees government above all as the most serious danger to individual freedom (and commerce) in society.

Almost all anarchisms recognize the close interplay between individual and community, and although some seek to eliminate or massively reduce this influence, most do not, but seek instead to make that interconnection one that enriches both individual and community, on the assumption that the best community is one where the individuals are not only autonomous, but caring of each other. Mutuality is an important theme here. One of the things that anarchism teaches is that each of us is rightfully autonomous; but from there it moves to the observation that, since everyone else is rightfully autonomous as well, I can have no presumptive claim to enjoy some good to the exclusion of another.

Liberalism and anarchism both start from the position of the autonomous individual and the principle that what is good for me is good for another, but each draws different conclusions. Liberalism decides that since we both want the same thing, and can't both have it, we should compete for it. Its social principle is that of *competition*; liberalism presupposes scarcity and the non-compatibility of particular interests. Anarchism argues that since there is no morally defensible difference between us, neither of us has any rightful claim to that good which is such that it excludes the other. The social principle here is that of *mutuality*. Moreover, liberalism approaches the whole question of the distribution of social goods in an essentially formal way, meaning that liberalism, with its idealization of reason over particular circumstance, makes decisions about the distribution of social goods, the application of law, etc., on the basis of a purely formal conformity to principle; anarchism has a more substantive approach, arguing that real people and real, concrete, situations must be taken into account. Emma Goldman's dismay at the outcome of the Bolshevik Revolution is exemplary of this fundamentally concrete orientation.

In some ways it seems that anarchism supposes a negative attitude: if we can't share it neither of us can have it. This is a bit misleading. What is going on here is that anarchism refuses to ignore what liberalism so often does: the fact that these autonomous individuals are not independent in the sense that they are outside of any community ties or considerations–they do not act in a moral vacuum. It is not only the case that all of our apparently individual actions actually affect people all around us, but that we are never individuals in the liberal sense at all. We can only be individuals in a community. The freedom of any individual is always bought in some sense at the expense of their community. I can only become an individual, much less the individual I am, because I live and have grown up in a community of human beings, in which I have been educated, cared for, employed, and so on. Individuation, it is worth pointing out, is a luxury of human culture. And, in a less than anarchist society, i.e., one where systems of exploitation and authority still flourish, it is even more true that my freedom comes off the backs of others. Consequently, I cannot indulge in the liberal fiction of a decision-scenario in which my choices are morally distinguishable from those that belong to all the other free agents. If I am interested in my own freedom, I cannot with consistency have no regard for the freedom of others. What I am is not just an individual, autonomous or otherwise; I am a member of a community, and the individual I am is a product of that community. And this is why anarchism is so concerned to change the structures of a community as a means of ensuring that individuals can be truly autonomous; but again, not just so that they can be atomistic individuals, but so that they can be creative members of that community. The relationship is a dialectical one, which is why anarchism is committed to slow process, rather than violent overthrow: the anarchist revolution is necessarily gradual, rather than apocalyptic.

Thus it is only to be expected that Goldman will argue the following:

> *Peace or harmony between the sexes and individuals does not necessarily depend on a superficial equalization of human beings; nor does it call for the elimination of individual traits and peculiarities. The problem that confronts us today, and which the nearest future is to solve, is how to be one's self and yet in oneness with others, to feel deeply with all human beings and still retain one's characteristic qualities.*[13]

Goldman pays a significant amount of attention to the goal of self-fulfilment. This is typical. What anarchism wants is to make us better human beings, which is to say, more self-fulfilled ones--less narrow, constricted, self-denied. And it is assumed that this will make for a better society. After all, wouldn't healthier, more developed, well-balanced and creative people make better parents, teachers, doctors, and such than the sorry lot of psychically pinched humans walking about now? Part of what Goldman is referring to is also simply the capacity and the opportunity to enjoy life: anarchism does not have quite the same grim dedication to the revolution that Marxism has often had–the purpose of the anarchist revolution is to make life *better*, after all, and that means more enjoyable, as well as more just. "Emancipation should make it possible for woman to be human in the truest sense. Everything within her that craves assertion and activity should reach its fullest expression..."[14]

Theory and Practice

Finally, the third great anarchist principle is the unity of theory and practice. Simply put, what is developed in theory must be put into practice. One of the conclusions drawn from this is that *means* must be consistent with *ends*. This provides a significant check on the sorts of actions which are open to the anarchist revolutionary, at the same time as it presses the imperative to act. It is never the case for the anarchist that the end justifies the means, since the two are really not separate. As Goldman says, in connection with the Russian Revolution, "There is no greater fallacy than the belief that aims and purposes are one thing, while methods and tactics are another."[15]

The goal of anarchism is a moral reform or recreation of the human being; every action an individual performs contributes to, plays a part in, that process; therefore, any incommensurability between the two actually puts the individual farther away from his goal. The individual is himself the means to his own goal; if he degrades himself by taking advantage of any device that makes itself available to him, then he makes it impossible to reach his own goal. In effect, he puts himself (his particularity) ahead of everyone else, ahead of the community, and this is completely at odds with the anarchist contention that we are each of us worthy of the same consideration. Thus, there can be no Anarchist version of the Bolshevik Revolution.

In fact, anarchist practice has tended towards the creation of comparatively small communities, self-administered and largely self-sufficient, whether this is in the 17th century Digger colonies of England, or in the communes of revolutionary Spain.[16]

Also, the primary form of anarchist proselytizing has been by way of "propaganda by the deed": don't talk about it, just do it, and the example will inspire others. And although for some this has meant throwing bombs and political assassination, for most it means living the anarchist ideal in one's own person and in anarchistic communities.

A few additional remarks are in order here. The rejection of any form of power relation or domination has always made anarchists (with some notable exceptions, e.g., Pierre-Joseph Proudhon[17]) friendly to feminist concerns (unlike communism). This is made especially so given anarchism's ready recognition of the force of education and the family environment upon the development of the individual and their attitudes towards others (i.e., willing submission or assumption of dominance). The presence of relations of power in the relationship between men and women has usually been very clear to anarchism (one might look at, for example, the views on marriage of someone like William Godwin, an early English anarchist and sometime husband of Mary Wollstonecraft).

With the rejection of power goes the rejection of hierarchy. This opens anarchist theorists as well to the claims of ecofeminism, which attacks the hierarchical thinking which is employed, not only in relation to men and women, richer and poorer, but reason or culture and nature. For all Marxism's emphasis on material forces, its attitude to nature remains profoundly mechanistic, which is to say, objectifying and rationalistic, whereas anarchism has tended to be more inclined to appreciate the natural world for its own sake, and has sought in many cases to find ways of living with nature which celebrate it as a thing unto itself (Goldman), something from which we can even learn valuable moral lessons (Kropotkin). Although it was not her first choice for a title, *Mother Earth* was in many ways a very appropriate name for Goldman's revolutionary periodical.

Incendiary Speech

Theory is something that anarchists are generally thought not to have. It is true that coming up with a systematic, and oftentimes just a coherent, political theory in the works of the noted anarchists of history can be a creative challenge. The fact is that for most of them, anarchism was a path to be followed, rather than a map to be drawn. They were activists, not academics. So, for most, theory must be pieced together out of scattered political tracts and pamphlets, speeches and autobiographies. This leaves gaps, and not a few inconsistencies. It is not a hopeless task, however, and the difficulties are compensated for by the fact that, because their task was essentially activist, they had to be reasonably straightforward in getting their point across. And in Goldman's case in particular, what we have before us are the words of someone who said what she meant, and said it clearly, if also with a certain vagueness of practical detail about implementation.

In 1911, Goldman published a collection of essays that were largely drawn from her speeches and articles published in her periodical *Mother Earth*. It was an attempt to broadcast in a more concentrated way the same points she had been developing in public lectures for some time, and to try to reach a wider and perhaps more thoughtful audience than those who came to her lectures. Goldman was by this time a well known and quite popular speaker, but it was also the case that her talks attracted either the already committed or those who were hostile and or more interested in the spectacle of her fiery rhetoric and personality.

The discussion of theory to follow in this chapter and in the next is largely drawn from these essays.

Spontaneity and Alienation

One of Anarchism's little conundrums is how to sell itself as a political option when it cannot, in all consistency, tell what it will do down the road. Anarchism is an open-ended programme; one that is and must be open to being rewritten as the future unfolds. As Emma

Goldman explains in the Preface to *Anarchism and Other Essays*, Anarchists cannot say how precisely anarchism will operate in the future, because

> *Anarchism cannot consistently impose an iron-clad program or method on the future. The things every new generation has to fight, and which it can least overcome, are the burdens of the past, which holds us all as in a net. Anarchism, at least as I understand it, leaves posterity free to develop its own particular systems, in harmony with its needs.*[18]

We cannot now imagine the future free of external restraints–so how can we prescribe conduct for those living under conditions of which we can have no concrete understanding?

This contingency of approach has perhaps put Anarchism at a disadvantage in the public persuasion game as compared to the various Marxisms, which have been much more forward in stating what "precisely" must be done. Anarchism is simply not systematic in this way. As existentialists have also found, people in many ways avoid being the self-determined individuals they necessarily are, and are depressingly ready to invest their own free future with one or more of the available banks of certainty, whether it be a Church, Party, or (pseudo-) scientific Doctrine. Freedom, and the responsibility for oneself and one's choices that it entails, are daunting prospects to say the least, and it is so much easier to allow oneself to be guided by received opinion, whether that is provided by political figureheads and pundits, a morality that one does not question, one's family or regional traditions, the prejudices and fashions of one's social circle. The indefiniteness of authentic existence as compared with the security and certainty of bad faith is what persuades almost all of us to choose not to choose.

Goldman's frustration with this tendency comes out in one of the Essays, "Minorities versus Majorities". She argues that the inertia, cravenness, and desire of the majority to be dominated and absolved of responsibility is what is truly responsible for backwardness of ideas and political awareness.[19] In effect, it is a claim that mass culture is to blame for the lack of social justice and originality of thought. All people want is bigger and more expensive, not better; what sells, not what is original or that expands human experience. Never a challenge, if we can have more of the same-old. As she says, the "most unpardonable sin in society is independence of thought."[20] And, throughout history, we see again and again that so many of those that once opposed the status quo are quick to take the place of their erstwhile oppressors, and eventually become just as bad as what went before. Revolutionaries become reactionaries once they get a taste of power, and they are kept in power by the mass, who prefer stability, predictability, and conformity.

This leads her to the conclusion that truly revolutionary change in society can only be the result of the determined effort of "intelligent minorities,"[21] and will not come about through the mass, which "clings to its masters, loves the whip, and is the first to cry Crucify! the moment a protesting voice is raised against the sacredness of capitalistic authority or any other decayed institution."[22] It is not nearly so much those who feed off the body politic that are the enemies of social progress, but that great lumbering beast itself, which likes nothing better than to be herded and corralled, colluding in its own exploitation against those who would loosen the bridle.

So, what does Anarchism stand for, in Goldman's view? Anarchism, as she defines it, is concerned above all with establishing a basic unity in human life, both in society at large and within the human individual. It is about human flourishing replacing the experience and the mechanisms of alienation.

Anarchism is commonly rejected on two grounds: one, that it is an impractical, though attractive ideal, and two, that it is a philosophy of violence and destruction, and hence vile and dangerous. Goldman's response to the first objection is to claim that, on the contrary, Anarchism is entirely practical because it seeks to do away with the wrong and foolish, and to revitalize. As to the second point, it is argued that the most destructive element in society is, in fact, ignorance, which is precisely what Anarchism aims to combat. Anarchism is about thinking through every proposition for oneself; authority is resisted not only in its physical manifestations but also in the form of blind adherence to unquestioned opinion.[23]

Anarchism defined, for Goldman, is

> *The philosophy of a new social order based on liberty*
> *unrestricted by man-made law; the theory that all forms of*

Anarchism

> *government rest on violence, and are therefore wrong and*
> *harmful, as well as unnecessary.* [24]

Of course, oppression and exploitation were, at the end of the nineteenth and early twentieth centuries, most obviously manifested in the material conditions of society: class division, poverty, outrageously oppressive working conditions, limited suffrage, and so on. The struggle to establish labour unions, workers' rights, and even the vote, were at their height. However, unlike some other social movements, such as Marxism, and while admitting that the major evils plaguing society were economic, Anarchism maintains that the solution of those problems must be one that takes account of more than the material circumstances–the reconstruction of society requires consideration of the internal and individual as well as the external and collective. Thus, Anarchism approaches the problems of social oppression and economic exploitation by looking one step further back; it tries to figure out, not just what is going on and how it works, but what leads people to enter into such situations to begin with–what are the motivations, the human presuppositions, that engender exploitative relationships.

Goldman suggests that the individual and social instincts have been in conflict with one another throughout human history. Since the triumph of classical liberal theory, at least, we do tend to think of the individual and society as naturally opposing factors, and much of Western political theory since the seventeenth century has focussed on how to balance or control the competing claims of either camp. How indeed can we respect one fully without destroying or severely compromising the other? Nevertheless, Goldman thinks that these two instincts of individualism and sociality are closely related and could be truly harmonious if only they were placed in the proper environment, and not kept blind to each other's value. [25] Anarchism (and this may be one of the reasons why it is thought to be inherently self-contradictory) often supposes the possibility of a reconciliation or even synthesis between elements commonly thought to be irreconcilable. Anarchism is "the philosophy of the sovereignty of the individual. It is the theory of social harmony." [26] In this respect, Anarchism attempts a task that is also undertaken by contemporary Ecofeminism, i.e., the reunification of traditional dualisms. We think of individual and society as natural, perhaps even universal, opposites. But Anarchism (like Ecofeminism)

45

asks whether this is really true (and: what interest is served in having us think this way?).

Anarchism seeks to alter the presuppositions of political theorizing: it rejects the traditional roster of players and fundamentally alters the goal of the game. As Goldman argues, Anarchism, instead of offering yet another theory about the proper relationship between the absolute givens of God, the State, and society, sweeps all these to one side and demands that we focus on achieving unity in human life. Religion, government, and property have all stood in the way of an harmonious blending of individual and social instincts, and the ability of each person to both think and act for him or herself, to combine all the elements of human existence in her or his own. It is clear that, although she does not use the term, Goldman is talking about the destructive process of alienation. Religion, by its domination of the mind, alienates a person from their own thoughts, desires, moral judgements; government alienates one's conduct from oneself, in the sense that how one acts is separated from one's native desires and projects–one does as one is told, not as one wishes, and thus does not express oneself in one's own actions.

Elsewhere, Goldman argues that the "philosophy of Atheism expresses the expansion and growth of the human mind" whereas theism is "static and fixed."[27] Theism is metaphysical speculation that ignores the physical and scientifically demonstrable nature of the real world.

> *The philosophy of Atheism has its root in the earth, in this life; its aim is the emancipation of the human race from all God-heads, be they Judaic, Christian, Mohammedan, Budhistic [sic], Brahministic, or what not. Mankind has been punished long and heavily for having created its gods; nothing but pain and persecution have been man's lot since gods began. There is but one way out of this blunder: Man must break his fetters which have chained him to the gates of heaven and hell, so that he can begin to fashion out of his reawakened and illumined consciousness a new world upon earth.*[28]

Goldman is critical of the ways in which religions attempt to maintain people's adherence. Ecumenicalism she considers a sham:

pretending that there are no irreconcilable conflicts between religions in order to establish a common ground from which to oppose any atheistic tendencies in the masses. She states that it is "characteristic of theistic 'tolerance' that no one really cares what the people believe in, just so they believe or pretend to believe."[29] Hence the prevalence of religious revival meetings and popular evangelical charlatans such as Billy Sunday.

Theism insists that there can be no truth, morality, justice, or fidelity without a belief in the Divine to ground them. But the morality grounded in this way on a combination of fear and hope is always a home for hypocrisy and self-righteousness. Instead, Goldman argues,

> *Only after the triumph of the Atheistic philosophy in the minds and hearts of man will freedom and beauty be realized. Beauty as a gift from heaven has proved useless. It will, however, become the essence and impetus of life when man learns to see in the earth the only heaven fit for man.*[30]

As for property, "Man is robbed not merely of the products of his labor, but of the power of free initiative, of originality, and the real interest in, or desire for, the things he is making."[31]

Thus, Anarchism is not simply concerned with the redistribution of wealth, understood in terms of the material products of labour. Rather, "real wealth consists in things of utility and beauty, in things that help to create strong, beautiful bodies and surroundings inspiring to live in."[32] Like Marx, Goldman recognizes that work is a human need, not just to provide the conditions of bare physical existence, but also as the prime means of human, personal, expression. Consequently, people must be able to choose what to work at and the conditions under which they work.

> *One to whom the making of a table, the building of a house, or the tilling of the soil, is what the painting is to the artist and the discovery to the scientist,–the result of inspiration, of intense longing, and deep interest in work as a creative force. That being the ideal of Anarchism, its economic arrangements must consist of voluntary productive and distributive associations, gradually developing into free communism...*[33]

Anarchism stands for a social order based on the free grouping of individuals for the purpose of producing real social wealth; an order that will guarantee to every human being free access to the earth and full enjoyment of the necessities of life, according to individual desires, tastes, and inclinations. [34]

All this requires complete individual and social freedom, and hence Anarchism is utterly opposed to that great enemy of social equality: the State, the aim of which is the absolute subordination of the individual.

With all this taken into account, then, it is hardly surprising that Anarchism does not put forward anything like an iron-clad programme. The different specific needs and even temperaments of individuals and social groups, combined with differing concrete conditions (for example, a wide-flung northern prairie community and an urban tropical zone industrial cooperative), will call for the use of different methods to address different sorts of problems.

Still, what remains common to all anarchists is the "spirit of revolt...against everything that hinders human growth," as well as a steadfast opposition to any resort to the existing political apparatus as a means of effecting significant social change.[35] One cannot change the system from within; one always ends up with the State as one's master. "Anarchism therefore stands for direct action, the open defiance of, and resistance to, all laws and restrictions, economic, social, and moral".[36]

And what, exactly, does Goldman mean by "direct action"?

Violence and the State

"Direct action" is one of those classic slogans of the anarchist activist. It can mean civil disobedience, strikes, demonstrations, occupation, bombing, and the Attentat–assassination.

Goldman's views on political violence changed over the years. From a willing, if somewhat inept, participant in Alexander Berkman's attempt on the life of Henry Clay Frick, she eventually became more convinced of the value of Kropotkin's limited pacifism.

In "The Psychology of Political Violence", she argues that anarchists have, by and large, got an unfairly bad press on the subject of violence. The vast majority of violent acts attributed to anarchists have not, in fact, she argues, been committed by them, but have very often been the acts of the police. In any case, she adds, anarchist acts of violence are compelled by a depth of sympathetic feeling for those who are brutally oppressed, tortured, and killed. Anarchist violence is not the ultimate conclusion of theory, nor is it the result of the cold calculations of a political programme, but it is the spontaneous expression of outrage and sympathy.

> *Anarchism, more than any other social theory, values human life above all things. All Anarchists agree with Tolstoy in this fundamental truth: if the production of any commodity necessitates the sacrifice of human life, society should do without that commodity, but it cannot do without that life.*[37]

Whether or not we should take all of these statements at face value, we can at least be clear that Goldman's "justification" of anarchist violence is not utilitarian. She is not saying that violence can be forgiven because it furthers the cause, or even that it prevents further unnecessary suffering. Rather, what she says is that violence is an *understandable* sympathetic response to the presence of human misery, not that it is a praiseworthy strategy.

Though wrongly blamed for Czolgosz's assassination of President McKinley, she was one of the few who was willing to defend him, at the same time as she considered what he did to be wrong. At the time of the events at the Homestead plant, she had bought into the idea that the end justifies the means. She abandoned such thinking, but she would not condemn those who resorted to extreme measures. Writing immediately after McKinley's assassination, she states that

> *Leon Czolgosz and other men of his type...far from being depraved creatures of low instincts are in reality supersensitive beings unable to bear up under too great social stress. They are driven to some violent expression, even at the sacrifice of their own lives, because they cannot supinely witness the misery and suffering of their fellows.*

The blame for such acts must be laid at the door of those who are responsible for the injustice and inhumanity which dominate the world....My heart goes out to him in sympathy, as it goes out to all the victims of oppression and misery, to the martyrs past and future that die, the forerunners of a better and nobler life.[38]

Acts of violence committed as a protest against unbearable social wrongs–I still [in 1913] believed them inevitable. I understood the spiritual forces culminating in such Attentats as Sasha's, Bresci's, Angiolillo's, Czolgosz's, and those of others whose lives I had studied. They had been urged on by their great love for humanity and their acute sensitiveness to injustice. I had always taken my place with them as against every form of organized oppression.[39]

Much later, when she was acting as propagandist for the Loyalists during the Spanish Civil War, Goldman had to deal with the question of how anarchists could legitimately engage in acts of war. The crucial difference for her is that the Loyalists are engaged in defending a revolution (one peacefully arrived at), resisting the attempts of the Fascists to destroy the advancement of freedom that the Republicans had brought about. Passive resistance, while apparently productive in the situation of India, would in Europe simply be futile; only active resistance could possibly work. In Goldman's view, defence of the revolution and imperialistic wars of aggression are not the same thing. Besides, passive resistance is appropriate where the people are rising up against an entrenched oppressor; this is not what has happened in Spain, where the rebellion is coming from outside the popular movement. In this case, it is armed resistance or annihilation. Life is stronger than theory, she points out–whatever anarchists believe, the actual fighting of a revolution will necessitate hard choices.[40]

When Goldman's attention turns to the military, we find a similar ambivalence on the subject of violent force. Anarchists opposed the Treaty of Brest-Litovsk, which Russia signed after the October Revolution in order to bring the war with Germany to an end. In many cases, this had less to do with the cessation of fighting than with the ceding of territory (Finland, the Baltic States, and Ukraine). As for the

Revolution itself, although initially enthusiastic, on visiting Russia Goldman became increasingly disheartened with its direction and methods, and with the notion that a violent revolution could succeed. For Goldman, ends and means are inseparable, and the idea of forcibly freeing people is inherently contradictory. Marx once chided the anarchists of France with the observation that a revolution is necessarily the most authoritarian of actions, and that a revolution that would be otherwise was a fond and childish notion. Nevertheless, the logic of anarchism holds clear on this point: an anarchist revolution requires, indeed *is*, a moral revolution that takes place first and foremost in the hearts of the people. Without this, the revolution cannot succeed, but will simply reduplicate the structures it sought to sweep away, and the use of military or paramilitary force without this moral change will simply hasten the demise of the revolution. The use of force is a very bad last resort that can be at best explained, perhaps at times excused, but not ultimately condoned. It is self-defeating and anarchists must simply find some other way to bring about the revolution. Agitation, "propaganda by the deed" (i.e., doing as one preaches), education, are the primary revolutionary devices of the anarchist.

As for the military itself, Goldman holds that military life brutalizes the soldier. The discipline and brutality degrade the men; they are treated like convicts or servants, without a shred of human dignity, forced to live under the most squalid of conditions and to pay respect to "every passing shrimp of a lieutenant."[41] Military life teaches a man nothing that he can use anywhere else and effectively renders him unfit for any other life. He learns no skill other than idleness, and if he had some other one before enlisting, it will be hopelessly eroded by the time he is discharged.

A charge that Goldman particularly makes against military life is that it is likely to turn a man to male prostitution.[42] Relying in part on Havelock Ellis, she charges the standing army and barracks life as suited to breeding "sexual perversion", though it is not clear why Goldman thinks this should be so. It may be at least partially explained by Goldman's attitudes concerning what is "natural" in sexuality; we shall see her views on these subjects in Chapter 3.

Goldman is particularly critical of what she sees as a fundamental hypocrisy in the American attitude to its own military.

We Americans claim to be a peace-loving people. We hate
bloodshed; we are opposed to violence. Yet we go into
spasms of joy over the possibility of projecting dynamite
bombs from flying machines upon helpless citizens. We are
ready to hang, electrocute, or lynch anyone, who, from
economic necessity, will risk his own life in the attempt upon
that of some industrial magnate. Yet our hearts swell with
pride at the thought that America is becoming the most
powerful nation on earth, and that it will eventually plant her
iron foot on the necks of all other nations.
Such is the logic of patriotism.[43]

This is her main target: patriotism, and the deceitful way in which it is used by those in power to hold on to power and to extend their grasp. The Spanish-American War is a case in point. Patriotic indignation at the Spanish was carefully built up by the press and eventually had the designed effect. But, after all was said and done, it became clear that the real purpose of the war was not the liberation of Cuba from colonial domination, or anything of that sort: it was the protection of the commercial interests of American capitalists against those of the Spanish government. Similar causes can be adduced for the Russo-Japanese War as well.[44] Patriotism (jingoism) is used by the State to mobilize its people behind military actions that in reality are little more than police strikes on behalf of the private interests of capital–interests that would just as readily abandon the people doing their dirty work to unemployment and misery once the military adventure is over.

The other hidden agenda behind militarization is internal pacification. Goldman cautions that the pressure to increase military expenditure has nothing to do with the need to protect the State from foreign threats, but everything to do with growing domestic discontent and international spirit among the workers. States well understand that the people can be easily seduced and mollified by the right kind of display, and military toys are ideal for developing positive public relations. And the spending is enormous. It is an ultimately insupportable expense of resources and of human beings.[45]

If patriotism were, as it is claimed, the love of one's place of birth and childhood memories, Goldman would have nothing to say against it. So many of the workers of Goldman's day could have had little in the way of fond feelings for their surroundings–the mills and mines–but in any case, "patriotism" becomes a massive and bloody deceit, whereby the people of the world are divided from and set against one another, and for no better reason than to maintain the despotism that separates and oppresses them.

With the First World War underway in 1915, Goldman saw the United States going through the same motions as Germany had a few years before. The "preparedness" campaign was really just a jingoistic and opportunistic effort to build up a huge military force. All the talk about "America for Americans" is Prussian militarism transplanted into receptive new soil. But is it Americans that all this military might is truly meant to protect, or is it not really the privileged class that robs and exploits the masses in order to forge the weapons that will send the poor to slaughter for their masters' sakes?[46]

How is it that women, "the gentler sex," who give birth to their children in pain and danger, are so willing to send those children to the Moloch of War, "militarism, the destroyer of youth, the raper of women, the annihilator of the best in the race, the very mower of life."[47] Preparedness is about turning men into automatons–killing machines. And who is the military called on to fight? Fellow Americans–working people.

But what drives this? Is it an innate lust for bloodshed? No, it is the bottomless pit of military expenditure, "the cut-throat competition for military equipment, for more efficient armies, for larger warships, for more powerful cannon."[48] And once you have all this hardware, you simply have to use it. Military expenditure then swallows up every other resource, sucking the life out of education, culture, and science. Being that overfed a beast, militarism has to find a way to burn off a few calories–it must have or invent an enemy; it must find a way to kill.[49]

One of the ways that the State responds to individual acts of violence is by imprisonment: the criminal justice system. Goldman has harsh words for a system with which she had some direct experience. Punishment, as it is carried out by the State, is retribution–revenge legitimized, with the additional intent of deterrence through terror. The justification relied upon is the notion of free will; if someone chooses to do evil rather than good, he must pay the price. This is a justification that Goldman rejects as obviously discredited, arguing that it only continues to be adhered to because of the belief in deterrence–even though this, too, is plainly ineffective.[50]

Once convicted of a crime, the prisoner enters an unmitigated hell of degradation, torture, and monotony that makes primitive revenge look like child's play. Prison destroys the convict so that he becomes incapable of any other life than crime and incarceration.

Goldman, however, does not favour a rehabilitative approach to punishment. It is pointless; like "pouring good wine into a musty bottle."[51] Her reasoning is that "nothing short of a complete reconstruction of society will deliver mankind from the cancer of crime." People become criminals in part through biological and psychological factors, but the primary influences are social and economic.[52] We live in a society that generates crime. Anybody is fundamentally capable of criminal actions; throw that person into the cruel conditions out of which so many criminals are born and nurtured, and the outcome should be no surprise. How then do we rehabilitate when we continue to support the circumstances that make crime the necessary response?

Once again, Goldman's conviction is that nothing really effective can be accomplished in terms of bettering society unless there is a wholesale reconstruction of our interrelationships and a reconstruction of people themselves, by themselves. Reform alone can only have severely diminished returns.

3

Sexual Equality

One of the things that makes Emma Goldman stand out as an early feminist thinker, as well as a social revolutionary, is the fact that she is perhaps the only one to set forth a philosophy that accepts the body; indeed, celebrates it and its possibilities for enjoyment and the communion of two people. This is remarkable because the basic strategy in the effort to demonstrate that woman is the rightful equal of man has, since Wollstonecraft and up to the liberal feminism of the 1960's and 70's, concentrated on that touchstone of liberal morality: reason, to the exclusion of the body.

First, a little background. Liberalism assumes that the difference between us and the rest of the animal world is that we are rational, and especially that we are capable of organizing our behaviour and our interaction on a rational basis. This is why we are able to have highly organized political and economic societies and cows and sea otters do not. We do not need to be herded together through the application of superior force–in fact, the most efficient and stable societies are ones in which reason rules rather than brute instinct or power. For John Locke, the classic liberal theorist of the seventeenth century, the Law of Nature is Reason: Reason is that faculty with which humans are especially equipped (by God) and which is their best means to self-preservation–the Law of Nature commands us to self-preservation; reason tells us that it does, and gives us the means by which we determine how best to do so.

Reason also tells us, along with experience, that everyone is basically equal, and that our actions carry reciprocity. On the individual level, reason is necessary for freedom, since we cannot be free without the capacity for understanding (which requires reason). At the social level, reason informs us that law is the means to maintaining freedom in a practical sense.[1]

Of course, it also follows from all this that whatever or whoever is not capable of reason cannot grasp the nature of freedom which he is allowed, much less use that freedom properly. This, it was long assumed, was the case for women. And thus, the effort of liberal feminists, from Mary Wollstonecraft, Harriet Taylor and John Stuart Mill, up to the present, has been to show that woman is, at least in fundamental capacity, just as rational as man, and thus just as capable of citizenship, education, employment, public office, and so on.

What has so often gone with this, however, is a despising of the body and the natural (what Elizabeth Spelman refers to as "somatophobia").[2] There is a strong, though frequently unconscious, tendency in Western thought to regard the body as other than the true self, as alien, as something that belongs to the (feared) natural world: chaotic, out of control, treacherous, disruptive. When Descartes identified the self with mind and not body he was merely cementing an idea that has haunted us since at least Plato and which the Christian Church sanctified. We are not our bodies. We are *better* than that; it is animals that are *mere* bodies. And this "we" has rarely included women.

On the contrary, women have been traditionally associated with body, with all the attributes of the natural, which include irrationality and a subordination to instinct. Men, on the other hand, must learn to separate themselves from all that is "womanly" and outside the supposed realm of reason, especially emotion. Abstract individuality and the ability to segregate the self from the claims of sympathy and connection with particular others have become the defining characteristics of both masculinity and citizenship.

With this as the norm, for women to claim equal status with men has required them to demonstrate that they, too, can fit this profile. Women must show that they, too, can "rise above" the tyranny of the body and live the life of transcendence as spirit.[3] If our body-ness is what defines us as women, and body is to be despised, then it seems that the key to women not being despised as well is to redefine ourselves as mind, which is to say, not-body. Strategically, it has been vital for women not to be seen as physical, and especially sexual, beings, in order to be taken seriously as the social and moral equals of men.

But there are a lot of problems with this. One is really obvious: no one is mind without body. We all have bodies. We are all of us naturally evolved beings. We have to stop thinking of this as a deficiency.

Emma Goldman clearly regards physicality and the life of the body as an asset, and her criticism of the emancipated woman shows the extent to which the wealth of the body, and that of the female body in particular, is championed by her. In some ways, this foreshadows the later development of "radical cultural feminism", which attempts to revalue and re-centre the female body and experience. In any case, Goldman's feminism and her views on sexuality in general are a logical development out of her anarchist presuppositions.

Sexual Freedom

Goldman is profoundly appalled by a set of mores prevalent in America, which she refers to as "Puritanism" (or "purism"). This is a kind of background morality that values an exaggerated modesty, to the point of ignorance, about the human body and a falsely stoic suppression of human emotion. Goldman considers it to be a repressive influence that is responsible for a wide range of social miseries and for the stifling of American art and culture. And it is what is behind the occasional eruptions into public prominence of organizations such as the Temperance Union, Purity League, and the Prohibition Party.[4]

Puritanism inhibits the most natural human expression of beauty and freedom. And by utterly failing to understand those deep human emotions that it repudiates, it has the effect of exciting "the most unspeakable vices."[5] It is puritanism that has made the human body something dirty, something that must at all times be hidden. Its promotion of chastity is an unnatural expression of shame.

The burden of this attitude falls heaviest on women, and it does so with a series of double standards of sexual morality. First, it prescribes different behaviour for married and for single women. The single woman is required to observe a regime of absolute sexual celibacy, or else be condemned as immoral or fallen, which itself leads to all kinds of ill consequences: depression, inability to work, insomnia, and sexual preoccupations. Goldman adds, referring to Freud (whose lectures she had attended in Vienna), that this "arbitrary and pernicious dictum of total continence also explains the mental inequality of the sexes."[6]

At the same time, however, the married woman is praised for being a busy sexual bee, producing as many offspring as remotely possible, even though the woman may well be physically exhausted or economically incapable of caring for so many children. No matter her circumstances, though, she must not take any steps to prevent pregnancy, no matter how safe; it is considered criminal to do so.

The upshot of all this is that the majority of women are hopelessly worn out and can offer their children hardly any care at all, and this forces many to seek out dangerous backstreet abortions–and thus puritanism ensures the occurrence of exactly what it seeks to prevent. The same is true of prostitution, which Goldman describes as "the greatest triumph of Puritanism."[7] Although Goldman does not draw out the argument explicitly, the logic of it is implied in the preceding discussion. If women who engage in sexual activity outside of marriage are immoral, and are because of that made socially outcast, their only recourse is likely to be prostitution; puritanism thus manufactures the social evil that it decries and uses as evidence that it must be given more scope to control the behaviour of men and, especially, women. Needless to say, one wonders how these women manage to fall all by themselves.

Goldman is, of course, entirely aware of that other double standard, whereby a male is fully expected to follow his sexual nature and cat around, indeed it is accepted as a necessary part of his personal development, but a female must be as pure as the driven snow, at risk of becoming damaged goods. It is not, in fact, the desire or the activity of sexual gratification that leads to prostitution, in Goldman's view, but the persecution of those who stray from such an unnaturally constrained path. And the ignorance of sexuality that is enforced upon women in particular is no small factor in their being put into such a position that prostitution is their only remaining option. But, again, it is considered immoral, even criminal, to make any information about human sexuality available, especially to women.

This was a crime with which Goldman was eventually charged. From 1915 to 1917, Goldman launched into the fight for birth control in a more wholehearted way than she had previously. She had for a long time been a proponent of Thomas Malthus' views on the dangers to the human species of overpopulation. This now combined with her views on the socially destructive tendencies of capitalism and war and on the social situation of women.

The April 1916 issue of *Mother Earth* was dedicated to the subject of birth control. Goldman argued (on an evidently Malthusian basis) that indiscriminate and incessant breeding by an overworked and malnourished populace cannot but produce unhealthy, i.e., defective and crippled, offspring.[8] Secondly, she argued that, unlike the soldier, who has for ages done his duty by taking life on the battlefield and in return been "paid by the State, eulogized by political charlatans and upheld by public hysteria", women have given life without any comparable compensation.[9] But now, woman is awakening and refusing any longer to be "a party to the crime of bringing hapless children into the world only to be ground into dust by the wheel of capitalism and to be torn into shreds in trenches and battlefields."[10] It is woman who undergoes all the risks in bringing children into the world; why should she not have some say in deciding whether she will in fact do so?

> *Surely she should be in a position to decide how many children she should bring into the world, whether they should be brought into the world by the man she loves and because she wants the child, or should be born in hatred and loathing.*[11]

Because of this, and because constant reproduction has serious consequences for a woman's health, women must have knowledge of how to prevent pregnancy for a sufficient period of time (three to five years) between children to recover mentally and physically, and to be able to care for the children they already have.

But, Goldman thinks, birth control is also important for the social situation of men. Large families tie working men to their employers, because they cannot afford to risk being thrown out of work. "Nothing so binds the workers to the block as a brood of children and that is exactly what the opponents of Birth Control want."[12] More remarkable, though, is the following argument. There has been a change in the relations between the sexes, one that so far only affects a small minority, but which rejects a traditional male attitude to women. Up to now, woman has usually been thought of as

> *a mere object, a means to an end; largely a physical means and end. But there are men who want more than that from woman; who have come to realize that if every male were emancipated from the superstitions of the past nothing would yet be changed in the social structure so long as woman had not taken her place with him in the great social struggle. Slowly but surely these men have learned that if a woman wastes her substance in eternal pregnancies, confinements and diaper washing, she has little time for anything else. Least of all has she time for the questions which absorb and stir the father of her children. Out of physical exhaustion and nervous stress she becomes the obstacle in the man's way and often his bitterest enemy. It is then for his own protection and also for his need of the companion and friend in the woman he loves that a great many men want her to be relieved from the terrible imposition of constant reproduction of life, that therefore they are in favor of Birth Control.[13]*

Those who oppose birth control talk a lot about how wonderful motherhood is. This is a lot of cant, says Goldman, since so many mothers must also work to bring in additional income, which is nevertheless a nearly insignificant amount. And this is to say nothing of the thousands of unmarried mothers that no one seems to want to mention, but which crowd the factories out of economic necessity. Without methods of contraception, there are countless abortions performed, with untold numbers of women dead as a result.[14]

In conclusion, Goldman declares that she will never make peace with "a system which degrades woman to a mere incubator and which fattens on her innocent victims. I now and here declare war upon this system and shall not rest until the path has been cleared for a free motherhood and a healthy, joyous and happy childhood."[15]

Prohibition is another target of Goldman's scorn. Never so many drunkards, she charges, as in Prohibition towns.[16] And yet this is an interesting case. History has shown, it is true, that banning sales of alcohol, or placing a heavy tax on it, generates a thriving black market of bootlegging and speakeasies, whereas liberalizing liquor laws has been followed, in some jurisdictions at least, by a decrease in consumption. None of this is really the point, though. Clearly, Goldman opposes the Prohibition/temperance movement because of the hypocrisy which she sees reflected in it, and possibly also because she appreciates the aesthetic value of a cold beer. But her dismissal of it could be seen as being a little unfair. The motivation behind the temperance movement was not solely, or perhaps even primarily, self-righteous puritanical moralism, but a quite practical attempt to protect women and children. If a man drinks his meagre wages, comes home drunk, angry, and without any money for food, his wife and children are at risk of starvation, beatings, and various forms of abuse. Goldman seems to ignore the fact that Temperance was a women's movement, not (only) because American middle class women thought it their bounden duty to spread purity over the land, but because women, especially working class women, and their children, were put in real physical risk by their husbands' and fathers' consumption of alcohol. No doubt the movement was readily co-opted by other interests, but it also had a socially defensible goal.

To return to the question of marriage and sexual freedom, Goldman argues that marriage is an economic arrangement; in effect, an insurance policy with harder than usual terms, because one cannot simply choose to discontinue payments. More to the present point, however, is the fact that marriage and love have nothing whatever in common. If anything, the two are antagonistic to each other. While it may be true that some marriages are indeed based on love, love is never the result of marriage, and if two people continue in their original love for each other, it has nothing whatever to do with the fact of their being married.[17] Simply, a civic institution cannot create a human feeling where none already exists, and where such emotion does exist, a certificate cannot either sustain or enforce it.

The circumstance that young women are kept utterly ignorant of sex until marriage, on the thinking that it is only marriage that can render pure and sacred something that is evidently inherently filthy, has to be a serious factor in the unhappiness and even physical suffering of matrimony. Contrary to what the public may think, it is ignorance of sex that breaks up homes, and not the reverse.[18] In short, Goldman thinks that it is ludicrous that a woman must abstain from all sexual experience before marriage to a "good" man.

So, in the end, Goldman's justification for the greatest degree of sexual freedom is the desirability of the greatest possible range of human experience, as personally enriching and socially advancing. In sum, the puritanical attitude diminishes life, because it constricts the range of possible experience, and this makes us smaller in spirit. As she claims,

> *Every stimulus which quickens the imagination and raises the spirits, is as necessary to our life as air. It invigorates the body, and deepens our vision of human fellowship. Without stimuli, in one form or another, creative work is impossible, nor indeed the spirit of kindness and generosity.*[19]

Suffrage and Emancipation

It is a great mistake often repeated, most commonly by those to some degree or other hostile to the movement, to assume that feminism is (or must be) one thing. In fact, there are many different viewpoints and philosophies within feminism, from liberal to socialist, existentialist, radical, postmodernist, psychoanalytic, and on, including anarcho-feminism. The oldest and most familiar is liberal feminism, which has led much of the fight for equal (in the sense of sex blind) treatment of men and women. Its primary claim has always been that women have the same qualifications for public life as men and so should have the same basic rights and duties in civil society. In particular, women must be granted the equal right to vote. The struggle for suffrage falls within this tradition.

Now, Emma Goldman, although as deserving of the name of "feminist" as anyone, opposes the suffrage battle. At the same time that women were struggling, even dying in the cause, to get the vote in Britain and North America, she was arguing that woman's suffrage, or universal suffrage, is a fetish. More than that, it "is an evil, that...has only helped to enslave people, that...has but closed their eyes that they may not see how craftily they were made to submit."[20] By this she meant that women were working under the false assumption that getting the vote, getting recognition of women's equal civil rights, would be enough to radically alter the position of women in society, and would be enough to make them free. As an anarchist, she could not possibly accept such a view. For her, suffrage is not a right, but an imposition, one that is fundamentally destructive of individual and social freedom.

Her argument is not extraordinarily clear here, but the point is essentially this: by giving people the right to vote what one is doing is permitting them to participate in their own oppression, and furthermore, compelling them to recognize the legitimacy of that oppression. It is as if one were to say to the people, "You don't like how the laws oppress you? Well, they were made by your legal representatives, and they were democratically elected by the people in an open and fair election–in which you participated, and so you are legally and morally committed to accepting their decisions as your decisions." Voting is a con perpetrated on the people by those in power, to give them more power, and take it away from the people, who are thus committed, in return for their votes, to regard their rulers as legitimate. Universal suffrage just means the universal freedom to be exploited; it has corrupted the people and made them prey to politicians.[21] Simply put, a corrupt system makes people even more corrupt.

There is, then, no reason to cling to the romantic and silly notion that the inclusion of women into the political process will in some way purify it. First of all, although woman is man's equal, it is unreasonable to think that she can succeed where he has failed: she won't make things worse, but she can't make them better. Politics is unpurifiable: "all existing systems of political power are absurd, and are completely inadequate to meet the pressing issues of life."[22] Politics is inherently morally corrupt, which is only to be expected, given that it is simply the reflex of the business and industrial world.[23] Women are, in any case, just as capable of political corruption and, if anything, the economic parasitism to which they have become accustomed must make them unsuited to political decision-making. It has distorted her conception of and commitment to equality. Indeed, what these suffragists are largely interested in is equal privilege with men for upper middle class women, but not for the great mass of working class women–who are the ones who really need some effective means of levelling the playing field as the ballot is presumed to be.[24]

In addition, if we look at the political behaviour of women, what we see is that they have tended to support the most barbaric policies. Goldman cites the example of Susan B. Anthony, who counselled women to act as scabs during the 1869 New York printers' strike.[25] And she asks whether social conditions are really any better when women have the vote. The sad answer is that they are not.

Women, she charges, have always been the most fervent supporters of all deities, of religion, of war, of home ("this modern prison with golden bars").[26] Suffrage is simply the newest idol. And the conservative orientation that sits behind the demand for the vote is evident in the justifications offered: if woman is allowed to vote, she will be a better Christian, a better housewife, a better citizen–that is to say, a better slave.[27] At the same time, though, women, especially American middle class women, are purists and snobs. They demand equality with men, but really think that they are morally superior, and intend to make everyone just as pure as themselves. No surprise, then, that American suffragists expect the advent of their vote to produce miraculous effects on the political landscape.[28]

For Goldman, the whole concentration on the vote, and perhaps "rights" in general, is a mistake–a distraction from the real point. The argument is that the winning of women's suffrage is pretty pointless if all it does is to maintain the system of hierarchy, i.e., women get the vote, but the class system remains intact. Legal reforms are in a real, practical sense, irrelevant–they miss the point and change nothing.[29] In other words, what great victory has been won in gaining the vote, if one still cannot get a decent and satisfying job, live an independent life without selling oneself to be kept by a man, and so on. The ballot, she concludes, will go no way towards enhancing the condition of women. Rather, true emancipation is not in the polls or the courts, but in woman's soul. And this is a matter of ridding oneself of the internal weight of prejudice, custom, and tradition. Woman becomes an equal through doing and being, not the vote.

Emancipation is about being able to be fully human. This was the movement's original aim, but so far, thinks Goldman, the only results have been to isolate woman and deny her happiness. In reality, women have won only an external emancipation. The problem, really, is once again that there has been an attempt to solve oppression piecemeal, without going to the fundamental bases of oppression overall. Women want to be able to participate in society and develop themselves equally with men. But simply being permitted to freely enter into an unequal competition has indefensible costs of its own.

As many other feminist authors have noted, before and since, although women are now permitted to become doctors, lawyers, engineers, etc., persisting inequalities and prejudices make it much more difficult for them to qualify and practise, and they must also face the rigours of the double day. Small wonder that so many women give up on the dream of independence.

But for those who remain determined to be their own woman there is an additional cost, namely, their emotional wholeness. To remain independent they must avoid any risk of amorous or sexual involvement. To become pregnant is to lose their career; thus they must not allow themselves any relationship that could have such an outcome. The professional woman must deaden any sexual or maternal instinct. She does not, therefore, expand her possibilities, but narrows her experience unnaturally. The fact that opponents of women's emancipation painted such an horrific picture of the libertines that emancipation would produce didn't help. In reaction, the professional woman has felt the need to present herself as more proper than Caesar's wife, and has made herself into the most upright and sexually conservative of citizens, and thereby made her own life colder than ever before.

Goldman's discussion of woman's emotional life and the longing for motherhood reveals something quite unexpected, namely her surprisingly conventional views about the nature of human sexuality. It is very clear that as radical as she is, Goldman is no separatist. In her view, every child needs the love and devotion of both man and woman.[30] And it seems equally clear that she thinks that a woman is in some way incomplete without a profound heterosexual love–emancipation must include this, at the very least as a real possibility. Thus, she claims

> *Until woman has learned to defy them [her internal(ized) tyrants] all, to stand firmly on her own ground and to insist upon her own unrestricted freedom, to listen to the voice of her own nature, whether it call for life's greatest treasure, love for a man, or her most glorious privilege, the right to give birth to a child, she cannot call herself emancipated.*[31]

But this must be a truly egalitarian relationship. Goldman argues that men and women can and must be able to form "one perfect whole."[32] This does not require any superficial equalization or elimination of individual characteristics. In other words, Goldman does not envisage the ideal future as one in which differences are erased. The problem is how to allow people to be their own selves and yet in sympathetic harmony with one another. And so, for the relations between men and women,

> *the most vital right is the right to love and be loved. Indeed, if partial emancipation is to become a complete and true emancipation of woman, it will have to do away with the ridiculous notion that to be loved, to be sweetheart and mother, is synonymous with being slave or subordinate. It will have to do away with the absurd notion of the dualism of the sexes, or that man and woman represent two antagonistic worlds....A true conception of the relation of the sexes will not admit of conqueror and conquered; it knows of but one great thing: to give of oneself boundlessly, in order to find oneself richer, deeper, better. That alone can fill the emptiness, and transform the tragedy of woman's emancipation into joy, limitless joy.*[33]

Much of Goldman's language in talking about sexuality is couched in terms of "nature" and what is "natural". Thus, when she criticizes puritanical attitudes and conventions, she remarks that "human nature asserts itself regardless of all laws, nor is there any plausible reason why nature should adapt itself to a perverted conception of morality."[34] And in the above discussion of the perils of emancipation she leans heavily on some, not entirely explicit, conception of natural sexuality. We cannot be sure what that is, which is a shame, since her understanding of "perversion" is clearly also to be defined in reference to this "nature", as that which thwarts it in some way. One thing that does seem to follow from what she does say in the *Essays* is that she regards heterosexuality as natural, that the natural development of a woman's life in particular, but presumably also of a man's, is in a heterosexual union, and for a woman in motherhood, whereas homosexual relations pervert this development and are the result of unnatural social conditions (e.g., barracks life).

However, it is also the case that Goldman defended homosexuality during her lecture tour of 1915, and had earlier on been a vigorous defender of Oscar Wilde. She recounts that this did not go over well with other anarchists, who thought the movement was getting a sufficiently bad press without also becoming known for being friendly to perverts. As was usual for Goldman, opposition made her all the keener and she continued on her course, strengthened in her conviction by the men and women who spoke to her on each occasion of the ostracism they suffered and the misery of attempting to lead straight lives and to come to an understanding of their differences.[35]

In the end, this seems to be what it came down to for Goldman–whatever her own assumptions about sexual normalcy, what she could not tolerate above all was that a person's *own individual* "nature" should be denied and distorted by the moral prejudices of others. It is probably unreasonable to try to argue that Goldman was defending homosexuality *as such*. Rather, she was taking a consistently libertarian stand (not unlike her stand on an individual's choice to fight): homosexuals must be as free as heterosexuals to live their own lives as they see fit and without interference from pseudo-moral busybodies and from the State.

In any case, heterosexual or not, the sexual partners of the anarchist future will certainly not be married. Goldman's criticism of the institution of marriage is scathing. It is all very well for the social reformers to get themselves and the public worked up into a lather about the evils of prostitution and the "white slave trade", but the fact is that *all* women are treated this way. "Nowhere is woman treated according to the merit of her work, but rather as a sex". So, of course, she pays for her place with her sex. And that is true whether she is dealing with one man (as a wife) or with many men (as a prostitute). The difference is only one of degree.[36]

A woman's options are limited to the choice between marriage, celibacy, and prostitution. In any case, a woman's place and status in society are determined by what use she makes of her sex, or rather, to whom she sells it. Woman is treated as a sex commodity no matter what her class.[37] Prostitution is merely the particular eruption of a general attitude concerning the proper function of women which is prevalent throughout society, one that sees woman as defined first and foremost in terms of her sexual usefulness. As she points out, "prostitution does not consist so much in the fact that the woman sells her body, but rather that she sells it out of wedlock."[38] Given such a definition, it follows that her entire life will be subordinated to the demands placed on her as an essentially sexual being. Though, paradoxically, this also means that her own sexuality is largely denied, because it only exists for and under the control of others.

Marriage, supposedly, is for the protection of women and their children. But while, for the man, marriage is a lifelong economic commitment, for the woman it means condemnation to perpetual parasitism and uselessness, both individually and socially. Not even a middle class wife can seriously refer to her home as *hers*, since it is her husband who creates and defines her world. It is irrelevant whether he happens to be a pig or a great guy; the fact remains that she is dependent upon him.[39] She lives in *his* house and gradually, over time, undergoes a narrowing of her own thoughts, until they are identical with his, and a constriction of her own ability to think for herself. Eventually, she is no longer capable of doing anything independently. She becomes dependent in judgement as well as in the material sense of economic support (it is in this sense that marriage causes the woman's individual as well as social deterioration--she not only is withdrawn from the public realm, but loses her identity as a person as well). In short, married life makes a woman a bore, uninterested and uninteresting, a thing rather than a person.

For Goldman, this also reveals the hypocrisy of the marriage justification. How can one seriously claim that marriage provides protection for women, when what it really does is to make women incapable of looking after themselves?

> *The institution of marriage makes a parasite of woman, an absolute dependent. It incapacitates her for life's struggle, annihilates her social consciousness, paralyzes her imagination, and then imposes its gracious protection, which is in reality a snare, a travesty on human character.*
>
> *If motherhood is the highest fulfillment of woman's nature, what other protection does it need save love and freedom? Marriage but defiles, outrages, and corrupts her fulfillment.*[40]

Instead, a woman is forced to buy the right to motherhood by selling herself.

Finally, then, Goldman's view is that women must make themselves free and whole, not through illusory legal contrivances, but by taking hold of their own lives, themselves. The following passage states this as well as anything:

> *Her development, her freedom, her independence, must come from and through herself. First, by asserting herself as a personality, and not as a sex commodity. Second, by refusing the right to anyone over her body, by refusing to bear children, unless she wants them; by refusing to be a servant to God, the State, society, the husband, the family, etc., by making her life simpler, but deeper and richer. That is, by trying to learn the meaning and substance of life in all its complexities, by freeing herself from the fear of public opinion and public condemnation. Only that, and not the ballot, will set woman free, will make her a force for real love, for peace, for harmony, a force of divine fire, of life-giving; a creator of free men and women.*[41]

4

Concluding Remarks

What, then, can we say of Emma Goldman's contribution to social philosophy and activism? It would be hard to say that any specific advancement was a direct result of Red Emma's agitation. At the same time, it would be a mistake to suppose that Goldman's influence was limited to that small group of now nameless and forgotten turn of the century radicals, who saw the advent of the Revolution in every act of defiance by the workers.

Goldman's field of acquaintance was extensive. From Jack London to Ernest Hemingway and Ford Madox Ford, Bertrand Russell to Rebecca West, from Kropotkin to Lenin, Zinoviev, Malatesta, and Louise Michel, Jack Reed and Louise Bryant. She attended Sigmund Freud's lectures in Vienna. She lived in a period of astounding social ferment, at a time when people took ideas seriously and believed that words and thoughts could have practical consequences–unlike our own postmodernist skepticism about the validity of either truth or action.

In an important way, Goldman's example shows us that the rejection of transcendental, eternal, absolute values does not force us to accept the absence of value of any kind. Goldman's individualist anarchism rejects the imposition of value; each person must act within their own conscience and choose for themselves what they will value. But this does not mean that the content of those values must be arbitrary or solipsistic. There are values inherent in human beings as concrete, even natural, beings, to which we can respond in a positive, nurturing, way, or in destructive or repressive way. What is wrong with the State, with capitalism? Both crush the humane instincts in humans. Goldman denies God because she puts the human at the centre of the human universe; she denies metaphysical morality because she affirms what grows out of the earth.

And this points to one of Goldman's philosophical virtues: she does not play the dualism game. She is not an Idealist nor a Materialist; neither a hard-headed reductivist nor an unprincipled syncretist. And while Goldman is not always consistent, she is on this question. Human beings have bodies *and* minds, and the species includes men *and* women.

In the history of revolutionary thought, it is fairly uncommon to find the kind of emphasis on sympathy, love, beauty, and joy that we find in Emma Goldman. And in those who do value these things, it is not very common to find so much faith placed in science. It would be an easy and altogether too obvious move to try to claim that the stress placed on sympathy by Goldman is due to her being female–sympathy, after all, we are told, is a "feminine" trait. And there is some merit to the claim that Goldman "feminized" Anarchism. But we find the same sort of emphasis placed on sympathy in David Hume, who makes it the foundation of all social morality.[1] (Hume, too, repudiates the sharp distinction made between reason and emotion in morality.) What Goldman really did for Anarchism was to re-emphasize its perspective. She did not repudiate theory; she reminded theorists of what the point was of the theorizing. Hence the "quotation" at the opening of this book: if the revolution does not make life better for human beings, i.e., not just more *correct*, but more *enjoyable*, what is the point?

It is worth saying, as well, that social revolutionaries have tended to be on the conservative side when it comes to the status of women. For example, Lenin's infamous letter to Clara Zetkin chiding her for wasting valuable revolutionary time on trivial matters about women, marriage, and sex instead of battling counter-revolutionaries.[2] Goldman put the "woman question" at the front of anarchist theory and practice. It was *not* a detail to be settled later, after the revolution: it was at the heart of the revolution itself.

Many of Goldman's theoretical initiatives were not developed much past a very preliminary stage. Her comments about homosexuality are a particular case in point. For the time and place, perhaps it is remarkable that it is raised at all, much less that she offers the defence that she does. Still, and for all Goldman's advancement on the whole subject of sexual freedom, the theoretical basis of her views is, all in all, somewhat lacking in either depth or originality. She envisages a relationship between men and women that is from a political and economic standpoint revolutionary (because libertarian and egalitarian), but her vision of how individuals will interpret their sexual feelings is in many ways conservative.

Because of this, it seems that her significance as feminist is to be seen primarily in terms of her activism and her critique of existing conventions and conceptions of woman's social role. Obviously, her rejection of suffrage as a solution for all the economic and social ills facing womankind puts her well outside the "mainstream" of the historical struggle for women's equality. At the same time, it provides a valuable critique of the assumptions being made by those who see the solution entirely in terms of an adjustment of the political structure, a critiques that was not seriously revisited until the 1970's.

In Søren Kierkegaard's *Two Ages* there is a description of something he refers to as "genuine community". When individuals in a community are each one related themselves to an idea, and only then to each other, then there can be a true community between them. Without this, there is simply herd-like behaviour, replete with mindlessness and meanness.[3] His point can be applied here, too.

Goldman's insistence on individualism was based in her conviction that an ideal is only a hollow stick for beating others with if it is not consciously chosen by each individual. Anarchism must not go the way of Communism of the Bolshevik sort–if the ideal rules the individual, Anarchism is lost; if the individual abandons the community, we have despotism (and capitalism). Goldman is trying to negotiate a fine balance between what she sees as two fundamental human instincts: the social and the individual, without sacrificing the one to the other.

Did she succeed? You tell me.

Notes

Chapter 1: Red Emma

1. *Living My Life*, 56.
2. ibid., 20.
3. ibid., 24-25.
4. ibid., 8-9.
5. ibid., 10.
6. ibid., 40.
7. ibid., 41.
8. ibid., 52-3.
9. ibid., 53.
10. ibid., 72-3.
11. ibid., 74-8.
12. ibid., 83.
13. ibid., 84-5.
14. ibid., 85.
15. ibid., 86.
16. ibid., 87.

17. ibid., 91-5.
18. ibid., 105.
19. ibid., 123.
20. ibid., 148.
21. ibid., 157.
22. ibid., 162.
23. ibid., 172.
24. ibid., 173.
25. ibid., 185.
26. ibid., 186.
27. ibid., 187.
28. ibid., 268.
29. ibid., 273.
30. ibid., 301.
31. ibid., 306.
32. ibid., 310.
33. ibid., 323-4.
34. ibid., 316.
35. ibid., 552-3.
36. ibid., 553-4.
37. ibid., 569
38. ibid., 570.
39. ibid., 587.
40. ibid., 591.
41. ibid., 597-8.
42. ibid., 598.
43. ibid., 599.
44. ibid., 604.
45. ibid., 605-6.
46. ibid., 608-9.

47. ibid., 613-23.

48. *My Disillusionment in Russia*, 21.

49. ibid., 21.

50. ibid., 25.

51. ibid., 29-30.

52. ibid., 46-7.

53. ibid., 50-51.

54. ibid., 54-6.

55. ibid., 207.

56. ibid., 223

57. *My Further Disillusionment in Russia*, 11-12.

58. ibid., 67-8.

59. ibid., 69-70.

60. ibid., 74.

61. ibid., 88-9.

62. ibid., 31-2.

63. ibid., 156-7.

64. ibid., 160.

65. ibid., 128.

66. ibid., 168.

67. ibid., 171.

68. ibid., 172.

69. ibid., 175-6.

70. *Living My Life*, 929.

71. ibid., 981.

72. ibid., 986-93.

Chapter 2: Anarchism

1. Stirner, *The Ego and His Own*, 183.
2. ibid., 184.
3. ibid., 168-71.
4. ibid., 174-6.
5. ibid., 194.
6. "Anarchist Morality", in *Kropotkin's Revolutionary Pamphlets*, 95-6
7. *Ethics*, 8-9.
8. ibid., 15-17.
9. ibid., 22-3.
10. ibid., 30-31
11. Bakunin, 128.
12. *Anarchism and Other Essays*, 222.
13. ibid., 213.
14. ibid., 214.
15. *My Further Disillusionment in Russia*, 174.
16. For the latter, see Murray Bookchin's history of the Spanish Anarchists.
17. From *What is Property?* (269n.): "Between woman and man there may exist love, passion, ties of custom, and the like; but there is no real society. Man and woman are not companions. The difference of the sexes places a barrier between them, like that placed between animals by a difference of race. Consequently, far from advocating what is now called the emancipation of women, I should incline, rather, if there were no other alternative, to exclude her from society.

"The rights of woman and her relations with man are yet to be determined. Matrimonial legislation...like civil legislation, is a matter for the future to settle."

18. *Anarchism and Other Essays*, 43.

19. ibid., 70-77.
20. ibid., 73
21. ibid., 78.
22. ibid., 77.
23. ibid., 49-50.
24. ibid., 50.
25. ibid., 51.
26. ibid., 67.
27. *Mother Earth*, Vol. 10, no. 12, 413.
28. ibid., 415.
29. ibid., 412.
30. ibid., 415.
31. *Anarchism and Other Essays*, 55.
32. ibid., 55.
33. ibid., 55-6.
34. ibid., 62.
35. ibid., 63.
36. ibid., 65.
37. ibid., 107.
38. *Living My Life*, 312.
39. ibid., 537.
40. *Vision on Fire*, 219-21, 227
41. *Anarchism and Other Essays*, 137.
42. ibid., 137-8.
43. ibid., 136.
44. ibid., 133-4.
45. ibid., 130-33.
46. *Mother Earth*, Vol. 10, no. 10, 132-3.
47. ibid., 333.
48. ibid., 336.

49. ibid., 337.
50. *Anarchism and Other Essays*, 118-9.
51. ibid., 121.
52. ibid., 115.

Chapter 3: Sexual Freedom

1. See Locke's *Second Treatise of Civil Government*.
2. In "Woman as Body".
3. Simone de Beauvoir is a particularly good example of this tendency.
4. *Anarchism and Other Essays*, 169-70.
5. ibid., 170.
6. ibid., 172.
7. ibid., 173.
8. *Mother Earth*, Vol. 11, no. 2, 469.
9. ibid., 469-70.
10. ibid., 470.
11. ibid., 470.
12. ibid., 470.
13. ibid., 471.
14. ibid., 472.
15. ibid., 475.
16. *Anarchism and Other Essays*, 175.
17. ibid., 227.
18. ibid., 231.
19. ibid., 176.
20. ibid., 197.
21. ibid., 197-8.

22. ibid., 199.

23. ibid., 215.

24. ibid., 205-6.

25. ibid., 207.

26. ibid., 196.

27. ibid., 197.

28. ibid., 203, 208.

29. ibid., 206.

30. ibid., 219.

31. ibid., 222.

32. ibid., 213.

33. ibid., 224-5.

34. ibid., 185.

35. *Living My Life*, 555-56.

36. *Anarchism and Other Essays*, 179.

37. ibid., 184.

38. ibid., 184-5.

39. ibid., 234.

40. ibid., 235.

41. ibid., 211.

Concluding Remarks

1. See Hume's *Enquiry Concerning the Principles of Morals*.

2. Lenin, 101

3. Kierkegaard, 60-61.

Bibliography

Bakunin, Mikhail. *The Political Philosophy of Bakunin: Scientific Anarchism.* Trans. G.P. Maximoff. New York: The Free Press, 1953.

Berkman, Alexander. *Prison Memoirs of an Anarchist.* Pittsburgh: Frontier Press, 1970.

Bookchin, Murray. *The Spanish Anarchists.* New York: Harper & Row, 1977.

De Beauvoir, Simone. *The Second Sex.* Trans. H. M. Parshley. New York: Alfred A. Knopf, 1952.

Goldman, Emma. *Anarchism and Other Essays.* New York: Dover Publications, Inc., 1969.

Living My Life. New York: Dover Publications, Inc., 1970.

My Disillusionment in Russia. New York: Doubleday, Page & Company, 1923.

My Further Disillusionment in Russia. New York: Doubleday, Page & Company, 1924.

Mother Earth Bulletin. New York: Greenwood Reprint Corporation, 1968.

Vision on Fire: Emma Goldman on the Spanish Revolution. Ed. David Porter. New Paltz, N.Y.: Commonground Press, 1983.

Hume, David. *An Enquiry Concerning the Principles of Morals.* Oxford: Oxford University Press, 1975.

Kierkegaard, Søren. *Two Ages.* Trans. Howard V. Hong and Edna H. Hong. Princeton: Princeton University Press, 1978.

81

Bibliography

Kropotkin, Petr. *Kropotkin's Revolutionary Pamphlets*. Ed. Roger N. Baldwin. New York: Benjamin Blom, 1968 (1927).
Ethics. Dorchester: Prism Press.
Mutual Aid. Boston: Porter Sargent Publishers, Inc.

Lenin, Vladimir Ilich. *The Emancipation of Women: From the Writings of V. I. Lenin*. New York: International Publishers, 1934.

Locke, John. *Two Treatises of Government*. Cambridge: Cambridge University Press, 1960.

Proudhon, Pierre-Joseph. *What is Property; An Inquiry into the Principle of Right and of Government*. Trans. Benjamin R. Tucker. New York: Humboldt Publishing Co., 1890.

Spelman, Elizabeth. "Woman as Body: Ancient and Contemporary Views". *Feminist Studies* 8, no.1 (Spring 1982): 109-131.

Solomon, Martha. *Emma Goldman*. Boston: G. K. Hall & Co., 1987.

Stirner, Max. *The Ego and His Own*. Trans. Steven T. Byington. Ed. John Carroll. New York: Harper & Row, 1971.

Tolstoy, Leo. *What is to be Done? & Life*. New York: Charles Scribner's Sons, 1913.
The Kingdom of God is Within You. New York: Charles Scribner's Sons, 1913.
The Law of Love and the Law of Violence. Trans. Mary Koutouzow Tolstoy. U.S.A.: Holt, Rinehart and Winston, 1970.

Winstanley, Gerrard. *Works*. Ed. George H. Sabine. New York: Cornell University Press, 1941.